CIVIL WAR TOUR OF
CHARLESTON

DAVID D'ARCY
Photography by Ben Mammina

Schiffer Publishing Ltd.

4880 Lower Valley Road, Atglen, Pennsylvania 19310

Title Page: The City of Charleston…as viewed from Fort Sumter.

Other Schiffer Books By David D'Arcy and Ben Mammina:
Civil War Tours of the Low Country: Beaufort, Hilton Head, and Bluffton, South Carolina
    978-0-7643-2790-2, $16.95
Civil War Tour of Savannah
    0-7643-2537-X, $19.95

Other Schiffer Books on Related Subjects:
Lowcountry Plantations: Georgia and South Carolina
    978-0-7643-3415-3, $29.99
Haunted Battlefields of the South
    978-0-7643-3385-9, $14.99
Ghosts and Legends of Charleston, South Carolina
    978-0-7643-3446-7, $14.99

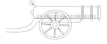

Copyright © 2010 by David D'Arcy and Ben Mammina
Library of Congress Control Number: 2010926156

Designed by Stephanie Daugherty
Type set in Engravers MT / Humanst521 BT

ISBN: 978-0-7643-3476-4
Printed in China

Schiffer Books are available at special discounts for bulk purchases for sales promotions or premiums. Special editions, including personalized covers, corporate imprints, and excerpts can be created in large quantities for special needs. For more information contact the publisher:

Schiffer Publishing Ltd.
4880 Lower Valley Road
Atglen, PA 19310
Phone: (610) 593-1777; Fax: (610) 593-2002
E-mail: Info@schifferbooks.com

For the largest selection of fine reference books on this and related subjects, please visit our web site at:
www.schifferbooks.com

We are always looking for people to write books on new and related subjects. If you have an idea for a book please contact us at the above address.

This book may be purchased from the publisher. Include $5.00 for shipping. Please try your bookstore first. You may write for a free catalog.

In Europe, Schiffer books are distributed by
Bushwood Books
6 Marksbury Ave.
Kew Gardens
Surrey TW9 4JF England
Phone: 44 (0) 20 8392 8585; Fax: 44 (0) 20 8392 9876
E-mail: info@bushwoodbooks.co.uk
Website: www.bushwoodbooks.co.uk

CHARLESTON MERCURY

EXTRA:

Passed unanimously at 1.15 o'clock, P. M., December 20th, 1860.

AN ORDINANCE

To dissolve the Union between the State of South Carolina and other States united with her under the compact entitled "The Constitution of the United States of America."

We, the People of the State of South Carolina, in Convention assembled, do declare and ordain, and it is hereby declared and ordained,

That the Ordinance adopted by us in Convention, on the twenty-third day of May, in the year of our Lord one thousand seven hundred and eighty-eight, whereby the Constitution of the United States of America was ratified, and also, all Acts and parts of Acts of the General Assembly of this State, ratifying amendments of the said Constitution, are hereby repealed; and that the union now subsisting between South Carolina and other States, under the name of "The United States of America," is hereby dissolved.

THE

UNION
IS
DISSOLVED!

South Carolina Secedes. *Courtesy of the Fort Sumter National Monument.*

DEDICATION

For Cayce, our friend and a cancer survivor... She exhibited courage, strength, devotion, and a love of life in her battles against cancer — just as the people of Charleston endured almost 600 days of constant bombardment.

ACKNOWLEDGMENTS

I spent much time at Lane Library at Armstrong Atlantic State University and the Live Oak Public Libraries in Savannah, so I would like to thank the staff of these facilities for re-shelving the many books that I left out during my research.

I would also like to thank Keira Davenport and Darrell Hearne for assisting Ben and I at our photo shoot during the re-enactment of the Battle of Olustee, Florida, in February 2008. The four of us were armed with five cameras and were able to achieve different perspectives of the action on the field.

From Drayton Hall, Natalie Baker and Peggy Raeder were at our disposal when we visited the grounds for research and photo shoots. I am also indebted to the staff at Magnolia Plantation for granting us access to their grand gardens, and would also like to thank Pat Kennedy for opening up Middleton Plantation to us.

Gratitude also goes out to Tom Churchill, who gave me directions and some background on some of the Civil War sites on James Island and along the Stono River. Richard Hatcher III, Historian at Fort Sumter National Monument, provided us with period images that enhance our story. Kellen Correia, of the Friends of the Hunley, provided much material that helped us tell the story of this ill-fated submarine.

Another great resource was the downloadable images from the Library of Congress and the National Archives, as well as the Charleston County Public Libraries website. I was also able to incorporate into this project the National Park Service's Soldiers and Sailors System, which allowed me to research specific military units.

CONTENTS

Preface.. 4

Introduction: Charleston's Early History 5

Section One: Touring Charleston... By Foot 8

Chapter One: Charleston's Soldiers and Politicians 9

Chapter Two: The Battery 21

Chapter Three: The Peninsula 40

Chapter Four: The Churches of Charleston 57

Chapter Five: The Market.. 71

Chapter Six: Charleston's Patriots 82

Chapter Seven: Prisons and Hospitals 90

Section Two: Touring Charleston... By Car 96

Chapter Eight: The Hunley and Charleston Cemeteries 97

Chapter Nine: Mount Pleasant................................. 103

Chapter Ten: Ashley River Plantations...................... 111

Chapter Eleven: James Island 120

Section Three: Touring Charleston... By Ferry......... 132

Chapter Twelve: Charleston Harbor.......................... 133

Works Cited and Other Resources 141

Index.. 143

PREFACE

I first visited Charleston in September 1992. My first weekend off saw me driving from Hilton Head Island to visit Fort Sumter. I would continue to revisit the city, bringing family and friends to the forts and to the historic homes. In 1994, I enrolled in a graduate program through the College of Charleston. I drove up once a week for an evening history class; usually I would arrive early and spend time on the plantations that dotted the Ashley River. Five years later, a friend of mine, Susan Bands, moved to James Island, so I used to sneak off and explore the earthworks at Fort Lamar.

In 1997, I was enrolled in a graduate Archeology course at Armstrong Atlantic State University in Savannah. My research topic was the discovery of the *Hunley* that was found in 1995, so I was able to research some of the people who were involved in that search. Three years later, I watched the *Hunley* slowly resurface on a CNN newscast.

In September 2006, one of the marketing experts from Schiffer Publishing wanted me to start on the Charleston title; I put it off because I was working on Civil War Tours of the Low Country and had been researching our Gettysburg project. A year later, I started to focus my attention on Charleston, revisiting the forts, plantations, and the James Island battlefields. My next step was locating period buildings downtown and exploring their histories. I spent the next twelve months researching the people and the structures of Charleston.

This book allowed us to be more creative in respect to the photography. Ben was able to introduce wide-angle shots for our story, and between the two of us, we took thousands of pictures, trying to find the perfect images. Photographic documentation was made easier by placing the photos and addresses through Google Earth and, for the driving tours, I used my Garmin GPS to log the mileage between the points of interest.

**Reliance on 'King Cotton'
enabled the path towards war.**

Introduction:

CHARLESTON'S EARLY HISTORY

The city of Charleston was founded in 1670 and endured two British attacks during the Revolutionary War. It was occupied in 1780. Charleston in 1860 had a population of 40,522 and was considered "the Cradle of Secession." To the South, the city was a symbol of freedom and, to the North, it was a symbol of secession. It suffered through a siege for 587 days — the longest in American History.

Charleston would serve as the place of the first confrontation between two American presidents; while both were strong-willed, only one could be successful in his war goals.

In December 1861, a fire swept through the city, destroying or damaging about a hundred buildings.

Charleston was not a target of the Union war machine until June of 1862.

In February 1863, the Confederate Navy Department authorized a plan to train a Charleston based Confederate Marine unit, commanded by Captain Thomas S. Wilson, to destroy, board, and scuttle Union ironclads. They were anticipating a Union ironclad attack on Charleston. They were to board the ships at night, disabling the crews by dropping sulfur, gunpowder, and wet blankets down the smokestack. With this task complete, the Marines would wait for the gassed sailors to emerge and surrender or die from suffocation. Training was completed and they were waiting for the signal, but the Union ironclads attacked on April 6 — the ironclads were forced to retire and the Marines' special operations mission was scrubbed.[1]

Charleston was a secondary target during the first three years of the war, as most of the supplies and troops went to Union armies fighting in Virginia and Tennessee. Fears did run rampant when Union troops landed on James Island in 1862 and 1863.

In 1864, Ulysses S. Grant took command of all the Union armies; his objective was Lee's Army of Northern Virginia and Atlanta, as supplies and troops were limited to deployment in the Charleston Theater. From that point on, long-range heavy artillery and the blockade were the only outside threats to the city.

By 1865, most of the Confederate coastal defenses had been stripped and sent to the main Confederate armies. Sherman's capture of Savannah cut off supplies that arrived from the South. In February, scattered Southern forces were gathered in North Carolina in an effort to stop Sherman from linking up with Grant around the Petersburg/Richmond area. It was decided that Charleston could not hold against Sherman's forces, so all Confederate forces in area were redeployed into North Carolina. Those forces surrendered on April 26, 1865 at Durham.

Many Charlestonians returned after the war...only to find their homes and lifestyles ruined.

An aerial view of Charleston in 1860. *Courtesy of the Library of Congress.*

CAST OF CHARACTERS

Confederate

Alston, Charles: Rice planter and Confederate officer in Charleston.

Beauregard, Pierre G. T.: Commanded the batteries that fired on Fort Sumter and served as commander of the Department of South Carolina, Georgia and Florida (October 1862 - April 1864).

Capers, Ellison: Confederate general who served in Charleston and with the Army of Tennessee.

Conner, James: Brigadier General who served with the Army of Northern Virginia.

Davis, Jefferson: President of the Confederate States.

DeSaussure, Wilmot G.: A Charleston lawyer and member of the South Carolina Legislature, he served as a Confederate general in Charleston.

Dixon, George: Confederate officer and captain of the *Hunley*.

Drayton, Charles: He enlisted in Charleston and later served with the Army of Northern Virginia.

Drayton, James: Enlisted with the South Carolina Light Artillery and served with the Army of Tennessee.

Drayton, Thomas: He served with Terry's Texas Rangers during the war.

Drayton, Thomas Fenwick: Planter and Confederate Brigadier General.

Hamilton, Paul: Confederate soldier and author.

Hampton, Wade: Planter and Confederate general.

Huger, Alfred: South Carolina state senator and Confederate Postmaster in Charleston.

Ingraham, Duncan N.: Former US Navy captain, he commanded Confederate naval forces along the South Carolina coast.

Jenkins, Micah: Brigadier General who served with the Army of Northern Virginia.

Jones, Samuel: Commanded the Department of South Carolina, Georgia and Florida (April-October, 1864.)

Lebby, Robert Sr.: Confederate Surgeon.

Lee, Robert E.: Commanded the Department of South Carolina, Georgia, and Florida (November 1861 - March 1862).

Manigault, Arthur: Brigadier General who served in the Charleston area.

Manigault, Edward: Chief of Ordinance for South Carolina, he later commanded troops in Charleston.

Memminger, Christopher: Confederate Secretary of the Treasury.

Pemberton, John C.: Commanded the Department of South Carolina, Georgia and Florida (March-October 1862).

Pettigrew, J. Johnston: Charleston attorney and Confederate general who was killed during the Gettysburg Campaign.

Rhett, Alfred: Confederate officer serving Charleston.

Ripley, Roswell S.: Confederate general who served in Charleston and with Armies of Northern Virginia and Tennessee.

Taliaferro, William B.: Brigadier General, he was in command of Battery Wagner in July 1863.

Walker, Cornelius I. W.: Charleston printer and Confederate officer, he served with the Army of Tennessee.

Confederate President Jefferson Davis viewed Charleston as the Confederacy's symbol of freedom from 'Yankee Tyranny.' *Courtesy of the National Archives.*

Union

Anderson, Robert: US Army major who commanded Fort Sumter in April 1861.

Buchanan, James: Fifteenth President of the United States (1857-1861).

Dahlgren, John A.: Navy Rear Admiral who headed the Navy's Ordinance Department. He later commanded the South Atlantic Blockading Squadron.

Drayton, Percival: This Charlestonian served with the Union navy.

Du Pont, Samuel F.: Navy Rear Admiral who commanded the monitor attacks on Fort Sumter in April 1863.

Foster, John G.: Major General who commanded the Department of the South (May 1864 to March 1865).

President Abraham Lincoln outmaneuvered Davis politically, forcing him to fire on Fort Sumter. *Courtesy of the National Archives.*

Gilmore, Quincy: Major General who commanded the Department of the South (June 1863 to May 1864).

Hatch, John P.: A Major General with the Department of the South.

Lincoln, Abraham: Sixteenth President of the United States (1861-1865).

Meade, George G.: Commanded the Army of the Potomac (June 1863 – June 1865) and the Department of the South (Summer of 1865).

Sickles, Daniel: Union Major General who governed Charleston early in its Reconstruction.

Charlestonians

Aiken Jr., William: Former governor of South Carolina.

Bee, William C.: Owned a blockade running company.

Calhoun, John C.: South Carolina Senator and former Vice-President of the United States who was a strong advocate for states' rights.

Chestnut, Mary: She kept a journal about the war.

Drayton, John: Physician who oversaw Drayton Hall and later Medical Director of Laborers on James Island.

Fraser, John: Owned a blockade-running company.

Grimke, Angelina: Abolitionist.

Grimke, Sarah: Abolitionist.

Lynch, Patrick: Charleston Bishop.

McCrady, Edward: Former United States District Attorney for Charleston.

Petigru, James: Charleston attorney and former state legislator.

Ravenal, St. Julien: Charleston doctor who designed the 'Little Davids' torpedo boats.

Ravenal, William: Owned a cotton exporting business.

Rhett, Robert B.: Owned the *Charleston Mercury* and attended South Carolina's Secession Convention.

Smalls, Robert: Slave who stole a Confederate ship, the *CSS Planter*, in 1862.

Snowden, William: Medical doctor.

Trenholm, George A.: Charleston banker and merchant who owned blockade-runners.

TOURING CHARLESTON... BY FOOT

Under constant long-range artillery that rained destruction during the last three years of the war, the Charleston area was a major objective of the Union war strategy. People were forced to evacuate the Peninsula in the fall of 1863. Prior to that, a fire had swept through the city in December 1861, destroying over one hundred buildings.

Chapter One:

CHARLESTON'S SOLDIERS AND POLITICIANS

STOP 1:
CHARLESTON VISITORS CENTER

375 Meeting Street
843-724-7174
www.charlestoncvb.com

Built between 1855 and 1860, during the Civil War this building was used as a depot for the Charleston and Savannah Railroad. Supplies and troops were shuttled along this line to all points between Charleston and Savannah. On November 2, 1863, President Jefferson Davis arrived at this terminal from Savannah to visit General Beauregard.

During the war, the current Visitor's Center was a depot for the Charleston and Savannah Railroad.

STOP 2:
AIKEN-RHETT HOUSE

48 Elizabeth Street
843-723-1159

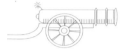

From Meeting Street, go left and cross onto Ann Street. Continue on Ann Street and turn left onto Elizabeth Street. It's the yellow house on the corner.

Built in 1818, the former governor of South Carolina, William Aiken Jr. (1844-46), owned this home. Aiken was also the largest slaveholder in the state of South Carolina, owning over seven hundred by 1861.

Though he was against seceding, Aiken did support the Confederacy.

Confederate President Jefferson Davis was a guest here in November 1863 and, from December 1863 to April 1864, it served as General Beauregard's headquarters.

The home was also used during the filming of the ABC "North & South" mini-series in 1985.

Aiken-Rhett House, circa 1865. *Courtesy of the Library of Congress.*

Built in 1818, this home was used for a time as General Beauregard's headquarters.

STOP 3:
NEW TABERNACLE 4ᵀᴴ BAPTIST CHURCH

22 Elizabeth Street

Turn right and continue south on Elizabeth Street. Stop at the intersection with Charlotte Street.

Construction on the church began in 1859, but the war slowed its progress. When the doors opened in 1862, it was suppose to have stucco on the exterior, but the lime was donated to the Confederate war effort.

The doors of this church opened for services in 1862.

STOP 4:
AIKEN HOUSE

20 Charlotte Street

Joseph Aiken served with a cavalry unit that protected the Charleston and Savannah Railroad during the war.

Turning left onto Charlotte Street, cross Alexander Street and stop at the brick house on the corner.

This home was built by Robert Martin in 1848 as a wedding gift for his daughter. During the war, Joseph Daniel Aiken owned this home. Aiken was mustered into the 3rd South Carolina Cavalry as a second lieutenant in the spring of 1862. The unit was assigned to the Department of South Carolina, Georgia and Florida — their main objective was to protect the Charleston and Savannah Railroad. Aiken participated in many of the battles that occurred along that corridor, including Coosawhatchie, Bluffton, John's Island, South Newport, Honey Hill, the defense of Savannah, and the Carolinas Campaign. Aiken surrendered with his unit at Durham, North Carolina, on April 26, 1865.

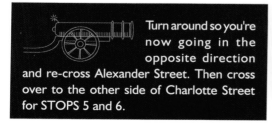

Turn around so you're now going in the opposite direction and re-cross Alexander Street. Then cross over to the other side of Charlotte Street for STOPS 5 and 6.

STOP 5:
PRIVATE RESIDENCE

29 Charlotte Street

Construction on the private residence began in 1815 by Richard Cunningham, but was completed in 1828 by John Gordon.

This house was used as a **Confederate hospital** during the war.

STOP 6:
GENERAL DANIEL SICKLES' HOME

33 Charlotte Street

Constructed in 1854 by Planter Thomas H. White, this house also served as a Confederate hospital during the war.

During Reconstruction, it was the home of Union General Daniel Sickles, who commanded the Carolinas' Military District during the early days of the Reconstruction.

Sickles was born October 20, 1819 in New York City and earned a law degree in 1843. He was admitted into the bar and in 1847 was elected to the New York State Assembly. In 1852, Sickles married and was appointed secretary to the United States' Minister to Great Britain, serving that post until 1855. Upon his return, he was elected state senator and the following year he was elected to Congress.

General Daniel Sickles, seated, was a former commander of the Carolina's Military District during the early days of the Reconstruction. Here he is with his staff after the Battle of Gettysburg. *Courtesy of the National Archives*.

This home also served as a Confederate hospital.

In 1859, he shot and killed his wife's lover, but was the first man in history to use a 'temporary insanity' plea to escape conviction.

At the start of the war, Sickles raised New York's Excelsior Brigade and secured a commission as its brigadier general. He missed the Peninsula Campaign and the Battle of Second Manassas due to politicking.

In the fall of 1862, Sickles was promoted and given command of a division. His division was not heavily engaged at Fredericksburg, as they were held in reserve. He was given command of the Third Corps in February 1863,

Citadel's Corps of Cadets trained Confederate troops during the war.

but never really earned any combat experience until Chancellorsville in May 1863.

During the Battle of Gettysburg, Sickles moved his corps forward from positions chosen by the Army of the Potomac's commander, General George Meade. His new position was the Peach Orchard, which was attacked from three different positions and flanked on July 2. Sickles' lost a leg to a cannon ball while evacuating the Peach Orchard. That wound kept Sickles from active military service for the rest of the war, but he was headquartered in Charleston during the Reconstruction—until President Johnson removed him for not adopting his policies.

During the Grant Administration, he was appointed Minister to Spain, and returned to Congress in 1893, helping to establish the Gettysburg National Military Park. He died of a stroke in 1914.[2]

STOP 7:
MARION SQUARE

Continuing westward on Charlotte Street, cross Elizabeth Street. Continue along Elizabeth Street; after you cross Meeting Street, turn left.

This site was formerly called Citadel Square and was the drilling field for the old Citadel. The building was constructed as an armory for possible slave insurrections, but became the military academy in 1843. The cadets went into service when the war began. Later in the war, the facility became known as Citadel Square Hospital and was occupied by Union troops after Charleston was evacuated.

Wade Hampton Monument

Wade Hampton was born in Charleston March 28, 1818; he later graduated from South Carolina College with a law degree. After graduation, he controlled the family's plantations in both South Carolina and Mississippi.

Hampton was pro-secession, but questioned the practice of slavery and the economic consequences of secession. After the firing on Fort Sumter, Hampton raised a military unit known as Hampton's Legion.

Hampton was wounded at the First Battle of Manassas, but returned to action during the Peninsula Campaign and received his commission

The Citadel was organized as a military academy in 1843, producing many able Confederate officers.

General Wade Hampton led the famous 'Beefsteak Raid' around Petersburg in September 1864.
Courtesy of the National Archives.

This monument honors General Wade Hampton's service to the Confederacy.

as a Brigadier General. He commanded a brigade in General JEB Stuart's cavalry division. He was again wounded in the fighting around Richmond in June 1862, but returned to the saddle before General Lee's first invasion of the North in September 1862.

He saw further action at Sharpsburg, the raid on Chambersburg, and the Battles of Fredericksburg, Chancellorsville, and Gettysburg. He was wounded for a third time at Gettysburg.

Hampton was promoted to Major General on August 3, 1863 and later commanded the Army of Northern Virginia's cavalry after Stuart was mortally wounded at Yellow Tavern in May 1864.

In September 1864, Hampton led one of the greatest cavalry raids of the war — the Beefsteak Raid. Between September 14-17, Hampton led a force of 3,000 that captured 2,500 head of cattle from behind Union lines. This was most appreciated by Lee's hungry troops. As the Petersburg Campaign dragged on, the lack of adequate supplies forced him to train his troopers to fight on foot because of a shortage of horses.

On February 15, 1865, Hampton was promoted to Lieutenant General; he was one of three Confederate generals to obtain that rank without a formal military education. He was later ordered to cover General Joseph

E. Johnston's Army of Tennessee's retreat through South Carolina and later served in North Carolina.

After the war, Hampton returned to his family's estates, which were ruined by the war, but he was able to turn them back into a financial success. He opposed the Radical Republicans and was elected governor of South Carolina between 1876 and 1878. Hampton was later elected to the United States Senate in 1879, serving until 1891. Hampton died in Columbia on April 11, 1902.

John C. Calhoun Monument

"Stripped of all its covering, the naked question is, whether ours is a federal or consolidated government; a constitutional or absolute one; a government resting solidly on the basis of the sovereignty of the States, or on the unrestrained will of a majority; a form of government, as in all other unlimited ones, in which injustice, violence, and force most ultimately prevail."[3]

~ Calhoun in an address to the Senate

South Carolina Senator John C. Calhoun was a proponent for Southern rights.

John C. Calhoun was born March 18, 1782 and began his political career in the South Carolina Legislature at the start of the War of 1812. By 1824, he was the leading supporter of states' rights and his speeches would inspire many future Confederate politicians.

He served twice as the Vice-President of the United States and it was thought that he would one day hold the highest office in the land, but he resigned as vice-president to become a senator from South Carolina.

During the Nullification Crisis of 1832, he led South Carolina's resistance to paying high tariffs on imported and exported goods. President Andrew Jackson had threatened to invade South Carolina, but cooler heads prevailed and the crisis ended in 1833.

Calhoun was the leading pro-slavery senator in the South; it was on his deathbed in 1850 that he argued for the South during The Great Compromise. He died in 1850 and was buried in the churchyard at St. Philip's, but in 1865, his casket was removed in fear of vandalism by Union soldiers and was reinterred after the war.

The Confederacy honored Calhoun by issuing a stamp of his likeness.

This building was utilized as a Confederate hospital during the war.

STOP 8: CONFEDERATE HOSPITAL

409 King Street

 From Marion Square, walk west to King Street and turn right. Cross King Street and continue north.

This dwelling was built in 1808 as a seminary for girls. During the war, this location was used as a Confederate dispensary and hospital.

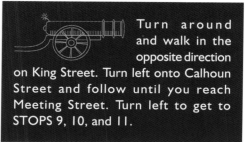 Turn around and walk in the opposite direction on King Street. Turn left onto Calhoun Street and follow until you reach Meeting Street. Turn left to get to STOPS 9, 10, and 11.

STOP 9:
SECOND PRESBYTERIAN CHURCH

342 Meeting Street
www.secondpresbyterianchurch.org

Built in 1809, the church cemented its place in Charleston history when they gave its bell to the Confederate war effort in 1862 for munitions.

STOP 10:
JOSEPH MANIGAULT HOUSE

350 Meeting Street
843-722-2996

"About fifteen minutes after being under fire, I was struck by a Minnie ball ... Which brought me to the ground. It entered in the back part of the ear, and passing thro & under the skin, came about two inches behind the ear & near the back part of the head. It fortunately was turned in its course by the high projecting bone back of the ear & making a slight grove along the bone passed out as I have described before."

~ Arthur Manigault
after his wounding at the Battle of Franklin,
November 1864[4]

This home was constructed in 1803. Owner Joseph Manigault was a planter and a state legislator. Two of his sons, Edward and Arthur, both served the Confederacy as officers.

Edward was born in 1817 and served in the Mexican War as a captain. After Mexico, he was employed as a construction engineer with the Charleston and Savannah Railroad. When hostilities began, he was assigned Chief of Ordinance for South Carolina, but resigned after a year. He later commanded troops at McClellanville and Fort Sumter during the monitor attack of April 7, 1863. In February 1865, he was wounded and captured at Grimball's Causeway on James Island. After the war, he served as a civil engineer in Charleston until he died in 1874. His journal of the last two years of the war in Charleston was published and is titled *Siege Train-Journal of a Confederate Artilleryman in the Defense of Charleston*.[5]

Arthur was born in 1824 and also served as an officer during the Mexican War. After that war, he became a prominent businessman and joined the 10th South Carolina Infantry in 1861. Manigault served with both the Armies of Mississippi and Tennessee. He was promoted to a Brigadier General in 1864, and was wounded at the Battles of Resaca and Franklin. The second wound prevented him from returning to service. After the war, he managed his rice plantations in Georgetown until his death in 1886. His journal, *A Carolinian Goes to War*, was also published. He is buried in Magnolia Cemetery.

This was the boyhood home of two prominent Confederate officers.

STOP 11:
CHARLESTON MUSEUM

360 Meeting Street
843-722-2996
www.charlestonmuseum.org

Founded in 1773, the Charleston Museum opened at this location in 1980. It has some exhibits of Charleston's experience during the war.

This monument honors the Southern defenders of Fort Sumter, 1861 to 1865.

Chapter Two:

THE BATTERY

STOP 1:
WHITE POINT GARDENS

The Battery was opened as a public park in 1837. During the Civil War, Confederate artillery lined the park to help protect the city from a Union naval attack.

In the confusion that erupted by the evacuation of the Confederate army in February 1865, some boys threw gunpowder on burning cotton. They spilled gunpowder while carrying it to the fire; the trail ignited and destroyed an ammunition depot. Also, over a 150 people were killed and many homes were destroyed because of the foolishness of the boys. Mayor Macbeth immediately turned over the city to Union troops, so they could restore order to stop the useless destruction.

After the war, the guns that defended or attacked the city were put on display throughout the Battery; plaques identify the guns and their place of service.

The relief on the stone base portrays the supplying of sandbags brought into Fort Sumter each night by Confederate soldiers and slaves to reinforce the damaged fort. The shield is centered with the state seal of South Carolina; the stars on the bottom represent the states of the Confederacy.

William G Simms, a pro-secessionist author, wrote the Southern response to *Uncle Tom's Cabin*.

William Gilmore Simms Memorial

Born in 1806, William Gilmore Simms was a noted Southern Antebellum writer and historian. He wrote about the Southern way of life and novels about the American Revolution in South Carolina. He wrote a novel in 1854 in response to the publication of *Uncle Tom's Cabin* called *The Sword and the Distaff*. He was pro-secessionist and his home near Bamberg was burned by Sherman's troops in 1865.

Hunley Monument

This monument was dedicated to the three crews of the ill-fated submarine that lost their lives in an effort to try and break the Union blockade around Charleston.

Homes along the Battery were damaged or destroyed by Federal artillery beginning in **August 1863.** *Courtesy of the Library of Congress.*

STOP 2:
A MIDDLETON HOME

1 Meeting Street

From the north side of White Gardens, walk to the intersection of Meeting Street. Stop at the northwest corner.

Owned by the Middletons, a wealthy rice planting family, this home was constructed in 1846, but was only occupied during the social season. It was used for parties and receptions from May to November each year.

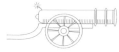

STOP 3:
COLONEL RICHARD LATHERS' HOME

20 South Battery Street

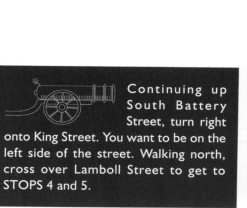 From the previous stop, continue onto South Battery, with the intersection of Meeting Street behind you.

Built in 1863, this mansion was purchased by Richard Lathers in 1870. Lathers was a millionaire who made his money in banking and selling cotton. He was born in Georgetown, South Carolina, but was living in New York before the war. Lathers served in the Union army and bought this home after the war, but he later returned to New York.

Continuing up South Battery Street, turn right onto King Street. You want to be on the left side of the street. Walking north, cross over Lamboll Street to get to STOPS 4 and 5.

STOP 4: ST. PATRICK O'DONNELL HOUSE

21 King Street

Built in 1856, this home was later purchased by Thomas R. McGahan, who was born April 18, 1825 in Madison, Georgia; he was a blockade-runner. In 1849, he left for California to find his fortune, remaining there for about two years. McGahan relocated to Charleston in 1853.

During the war, McGahan ran goods into Galveston, Texas. He returned to Charleston after the war.[6] His cousin was Margaret Mitchell, author of *Gone With the Wind*.[7] She based the character Melanie after McGahan's wife Emma. McGahan died in Charleston on September 26, 1905.

This home was owned by blockade-runner, Thomas McGahan, during the war.

STOP 5:
MILES BREWTON HOUSE

27 King Street

This house was used as Federal Headquarters during the occupation of Charleston.

Built between 1765 and 1769, this home was the Federal Headquarters during the occupation of Charleston. Federal Generals Meade and Hatch were assigned here at different times throughout 1865.

General George G. Meade, the last commander of the Union Army of the Potomac, was stationed here in 1865.
Courtesy of the National Archives.

Department of the South's General John Hatch and his staff after Charleston was evacuated in February 1865. *Courtesy of the Library of Congress.*

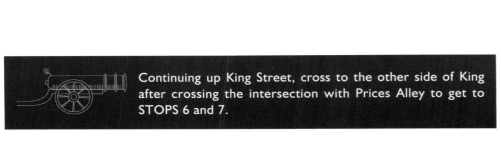

Continuing up King Street, cross to the other side of King after crossing the intersection with Prices Alley to get to STOPS 6 and 7.

General George G. Meade, the last commander of the Union Army of the Potomac, was stationed here in 1865. *Courtesy of the National Archives.*

STOP 6:
A TRENHOLM HOME

54 King Street

This private residence was constructed in 1768. Charleston blockade-runner, George Trenholm, owned it during the war.

STOP 7:
MARX COHEN HOUSE

85 King Street

Marx Cohen was a planter along the Ashley River and had this home constructed in 1844. Cohen's son, Marx Junior, served as a Confederate officer and fell at the Battle of Bentonville, North Carolina, in March 1865.

This dwelling was constructed in 1844. It belonged to the Cohens, a planter family that lived along the Ashley River.

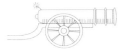

STOP 8:
BRIGADIER GENERAL JAMES SIMONS HOME

93 Broad Street

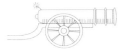 Continuing up King Street, turn right onto Broad Street. You want to be on the right side of the street.

This private residence was constructed in 1788 and purchased by James Simons in the mid-1850s. Born in 1813, Simons was a lawyer and state legislator before the war. He commanded the batteries on Morris Island during the bombardment of Fort Sumter in April 1861. He later argued with Governor Pickens, so he resigned his commission and volunteered in a Marion Artillery unit. Simons died in Charleston in 1879.

 Crossing Broad Street, the next two stops are BEFORE the intersection with Meeting Street.

STOP 9:
CHARLESTON COUNTY COURT HOUSE

84 Broad Street

Built in 1753 as the provincial capitol of the colony of South Carolina, the structure was gutted by fire in 1788 and rebuilt in 1792 with additions.

Soldiers of the 54th Massachusetts were tried and acquitted here after their capture at Battery Wagner in July 1863.

STOP 10:
CHARLESTON CITY HALL

80 Broad Street

 Cross the street. The building will be on the corner.

Initially, this building was constructed as a branch of the Bank of the United States between 1800 and 1804. The bank had its charter revoked by Congress in 1811 and the building became the Charleston City Hall in 1818. It still serves the city in that capacity today.

Behind City Hall is Washington Park, where three monuments honoring veterans of the Civil War are located.

City Hall during the Union occupation in 1865. *Courtesy of the Library of Congress.*

Constructed between 1800-1804, this building served as the City Hall during the war.

Washington Light Infantry

This unit was a pre-war militia unit that supplied three companies for the Confederate armies. The dead from the war are listed on the shaft.

General Beauregard

This monument honors General Pierre Beauregard's wartime service in Charleston.

Henry Timrod

Born December 8, 1828 in Charleston, Timrod later studied law at the University of Georgia. He was known as 'the Poet Laureate of the Confederacy.' Timrod published poems about patriotism that helped to swell Confederate enlistments early in the war; he too joined the army and fought at Shiloh. He was discharged and later served briefly as a western war correspondent for the *Charleston Mercury*. Because of illness, he couldn't serve the Confederacy other than as a poet. He died October 7, 1867, of tuberculosis.

A plaque honors members of the congregation who were killed in action while serving in the Confederate armies.

STOP 11:
ST. MICHAEL'S
EPISCOPAL CHURCH

71 Meeting Street

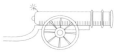 Retrace your steps and cross Broad Street where it intersects with Meeting Street. Turn left onto Meeting Street. The Church will be on your left.

"Dear Old Charleston, My heart is very sad. To leave her now to those wretches after she has so long withstood their assault. Indeed, indeed it is a bitter cup to drink, but if we can assure the safety of Columbia and those in it, we will not complain."

~ Corporal Augustine I. Smyth, of the Confederate Signal Corps. who had been posted in the steeple in February 1865 before the evacuation[8]

The church was built in 1841, but its history dates back to the founding of Charleston in 1670. Twenty years later, General Robert E. Lee worshipped here while he was in the city in December 1861.

Two Charleston brothers, Thomas Fenwick and Percival Drayton, prayed together all night before taking their assignments in early 1861. Percival remained loyal to the United States Navy while Thomas offered his services to the Confederate army.

In November 1861, Percival was part of the invasion fleet that attacked Port Royal Sound on Hilton Head Island. Ironically, his brother, Thomas, commanded the Confederate defenses on Hilton Head; the brothers never saw each other again. Percival died of disease in August 1865.[9]

During the war, the steeple was painted black, so it would be less likely seen by Federal batteries. The bells were sent to Columbia out of fear of Sherman's march on Charleston, but were damaged during Sherman's occupation of Columbia. After the war, they were sent to England for repair.

This steeple served as an observation post for the Confederate Signal Corps.

STOP 12:
PAYAS-MORDECAI HOUSE

69 Meeting Street

 Continuing down Meeting Street, you are now walking back to White Point Gardens, the Battery.

Moses Cohen Mordecai purchased this home in 1837. He opposed South Carolina's secession, but profited from the war through some ownership in a blockade-running company.

In 1870, Cohen, in conjunction with the Ladies Memorial Association, paid the expenses to bring back South Carolina's dead from Gettysburg; many are now interred at Magnolia Cemetery.

Constructed in 1837, a partner in a local blockade running company owned this home.

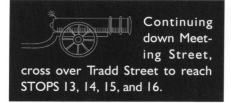 Continuing down Meeting Street, cross over Tradd Street to reach STOPS 13, 14, 15, and 16.

STOP 13:
FIRST SCOTS PRESBYTERIAN CHURCH

57 Meeting Street

The church gave its bell to the Confederacy, so that it could be melted down for ammunition. The bell was replaced in 1999 and a plaque outside the church honors those who died in the service of the Confederacy.

Though its congregation was organized in 1731, this house of worship wasn't constructed until 1914.

STOP 14:
NATHANIEL RUSSELL HOUSE

51 Meeting Street
843-724-8481

Built between 1803 and 1808, Governor Robert Allston owned the house during the war, but he and his family evacuated their home in 1863 when Yankee iron rained on the Lower Peninsula. Allston, who died in 1864, was governor of South Carolina from 1856 to 1858.

Evacuated in 1863 when the Federals started bombarding the Lower Peninsula, the house was able to survive the war.

STOP 15:
GENERAL BEAUREGARD'S HEADQUARTERS

37 Meeting Street

This home was Beauregard's headquarters from October 1862 to August 1863.

"It must be held to the bitter end with infantry alone. There can be no hope of reinforcements."

~ Beauregard's orders to Lieutenant Colonel Stephen Elliot, new commander at Fort Sumter, September 8, 1863.[10]

Constructed in 1775, this house served as General Pierre G. T. Beauregard's first headquarters when he was assigned to Charleston, from October 1862 to August 1863 — he was forced to move when the Union's shelling intensified on the Lower Peninsula.

Beauregard was born near New Orleans May 28, 1818. He graduated second in the West Point Class of 1838 and was twice promoted for gallantry during the Mexican War. In 1851, he was appointed Superintending Engineer of the New Orleans' Custom House.

Early in 1861, he was appointed Superintendent of West Point, but resigned after Louisiana seceded. Within a month, he was offered the rank of Brigadier General with the new Confederate Army and commanded the forces that fired on Fort Sumter in April 1861; later that year, he helped in the Confederate victory at First Manassas.

In April 1862, Beauregard took over command of the Army of Mississippi after General Albert S. Johnston was mortally wounded at the Battle of Shiloh.

After Shiloh, Beauregard bounced around to different departmental commands around the Confederate States; the Department of South Carolina, Georgia, and Florida; the Department of North Carolina and Southeastern Virginia; and he commanded some forces that opposed Sherman in North Carolina in 1865.

After the war, he was President of the New Orleans, Jackson and Mississippi Railroad. He also supervised the Louisiana Lottery and was the Commissioner of Public Works in New Orleans. Beauregard died in New Orleans February 20, 1893.

General Beauregard commanded the Confederate guns that fired at Fort Sumter on April 12, 1861.
Courtesy of the National Archives.

STOP 16:
DANIEL E. HUGER HOUSE

34 Meeting Street

This house was constructed in 1768. Homeowner Daniel Huger served in the United States Senate from 1845 to 1850.

Damaged during the Union's shelling, Union soldiers then looted the house during their occupation of it.

STOP 17:
DRAYTON HOME

2 Ladson Street

Continuing down Meeting Street, turn right onto Ladson Street.

Constructed in 1746, this home was used for social gatherings by the Drayton family, a rice planting family in che Charleston area.

Chapter Three:
THE PENINSULA

"It would appear, Sir, that despairing of reducing these works, you now resort to the novel measure of turning your guns against old men, the women and children, and the hospitals of a sleeping city — an act of inexcusable barbarity."

General Beauregard's answer to Gilmore's demand that Sumter and Morris Island be evacuated, August 21, 1863[11]

General Quincy Gilmore was in command of Union operations against Charleston in the summer of 1863. Gilmore threatened to fire on Charleston if it wasn't evacuated — and the Swamp Angel did fire into the city as did additional Union guns. Heavy shelling would later force the evacuation of this part of the city. *Courtesy of the National Archives.*

STOP 1: SNOWDEN HOUSE

15 Church Street

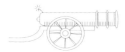 Returning to Meeting Street, turn right and walk to White Point Gardens. From there, cross South Battery Street onto Church Street.

Constructed in 1842, Dr. William Snowden and his wife, Amarinthia, owned this home during the war, which was eventually used as a Confederate Hospital.

The Snowdens evacuated the house in 1864 after Union shelling intensified on the Peninsula, but returned after the war. They helped to raise money for the Confederate monument in Margolia Cemetery.

The Ladies Memorial Association held their meetings at this home. The forerunner of the United Daughters of the Confederacy, the Association raised money so they could bring back South Carolina's dead from Gettysburg during the early 1870s.

STOP 2: GENERAL ELLISON CAPERS HOME

69 Church Street

 Continue up Church Street. At the Water Street intersection, Church Street veers to the right.

Ellison Capers was born in Charleston October 14, 1837 and graduated from the South Carolina Military Academy, the Citadel, in 1857. During the bombardment of Fort Sumter, he served as an officer on Sullivan's Island. He soon helped organize the 24th South Carolina Infantry and fought with that unit as a major during the Battle of Secessionville in June 1862. After Secessionville, he served in both of the Carolinas and was soon promoted to colonel.

In 1863, Capers and his regiment were ordered to join the Army of Tennessee near Tullahoma, Tennessee. He fought at Chickamauga, Chattanooga, and Atlanta, and was promoted to Brigadier General in November 1864 after the Battle of Franklin.

After the war, he was the South Carolina Secretary of State, a chaplain for the United Confederate Veterans, and an Episcopal Bishop. He died in Columbia April 22, 1908 and is buried in the Trinity Churchyard.[12]

This was the home of Confederate General Ellison Capers, who served in South Carolina and with the Army of Tennessee.

STOP 3:
HEYWARD-WASHINGTON HOUSE

87 Church Street

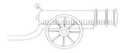

Continuing up Church Street, cross over Tradd Street to get to this house.

This house was built in 1772. Before the war, it was the home of sisters Sarah and Angelina Grimke, who lived here with twelve other siblings and slaves. Their family owned a plantation in Beaufort; both women were educated in the North and were active in the abolitionist movement.

Angelina married Theodore Weld, a prominent abolitionist leader.

Angelina and Sarah were both very vocal, lecturing for the Anti-Slavery Society, because of their beliefs — the Charleston police were ordered to arrest them if they ever returned to the city[14] — and they both supported Abraham Lincoln during the 1860 presidential campaign.

Sarah Grimke, responding to men who did not wish to have women lecture at the Anti-Slavery Society meetings, said that men were attempting to "drive women from almost every sphere of moral action" and called on women "to rise from that degradation and bondage to which the faculties of our minds have been prevented from expanding to their full growth and are sometimes wholly crushed."[13]

Sara and Angelina then both later became active in the rights of women.

Two abolitionist sisters, Sarah and Angelina Grimke, lived here before receiving their education in the North.

STOP 4:
JAMES LOUIS PETIGRU'S LAW OFFICE

8 St. Michaels Alley

 Continue up Church Street and turn left onto St. Michaels Alley.

"South Carolina is too small for a Republic and too large for an insane asylum."

~ Petigru, after South Carolina seceded, December 20, 1860[15]

James Louis Petigru's law practice was located here; he employed his cousin James Johnston Pettigrew. James Louis preferred the French version of Petigru.

Johnston Pettigrew was born in Tyrell County, North Carolina, July 4, 1828 and graduated from the University of North Carolina in 1847. He was soon practicing law in Charleston and was elected to the South Carolina legislature in 1856.

At the start of the war, Pettigrew was elected colonel of the 12th South Carolina Infantry and was promoted to Brigadier General in February 1862. He was wounded and captured outside of Richmond during the Battle of Seven Pines. Later that summer, he was exchanged and commanded some of the defenses of Petersburg and parts of North Carolina. His brigade was transferred to the Army of Northern Virginia just before the Gettysburg Campaign. Pettigrew took over General Henry Heth's division on July 1, after Heth had been wounded. The division assaulted Cemetery Ridge on July 3 and he was killed July 14, fighting a rear guard action at Falling Waters, Maryland. He is buried near Bunker Hill, Virginia.[16]

Confederate General Johnston Pettigrew practiced law here with his cousin before the war.

STOP 5:
DISTRICT COURT HOUSE

62 Broad Street

 Returning to Church Street, turn left. Continue on Church Street and turn left on Broad Street.

"The United States no longer had authority to hold court in South Carolina."

~ Judge Andrew McGrath, after learning Lincoln had been elected President in November 1860[17]

A United States Court House, during the war the building was the "Confederate States Court for the District of South Carolina." After the war, the building was used as a home for Confederate widows and orphans.[18]

The day Lincoln was elected President of the United States, court was in session and Judge Andrew G. McGrath was presiding. Upon hearing the results of the election, he stood up, took off his robe, and adjourned the session.

STOP 6:
THE WALKER, EVANS, AND COGSWELL BUILDING

3 Broad Street

 From the previous stop, continue walking on Broad Street, toward East Bay Street, and turn right.

Constructed between 1853 and 1854, this building was used for printing operations, but it was relocated to Columbia in 1863.[19] They printed military forms and Confederate currency.

One of the partners, Lieutenant Colonel Cornelius Irvine Walker, commanded the 10th South Carolina Infantry and was elected captain of the unit when it was organized at Georgetown in July 1861. Initially, they were attached to the Department of South Carolina, Georgia, and Florida, but were later reassigned to the Southern forces gathering in Mississippi in March 1862. That autumn the 10th was transferred to the Army of Tennessee.

Walker fought with the regiment from Perryville to the army's surrender at North Carolina in April 1865. He was wounded twice: first around Atlanta in July 1864 and again at Kingston, North Carolina, in March 1865.[20]

After the war, Walker became the Commander-in-Chief of the United Confederate Veterans. He also wrote a history of the 10th South Carolina Infantry and is buried in the St. Phillip's Churchyard in a grave filled with earth from the Chickamauga Battlefield.

This printing office produced military forms and Confederate currency.

STOP 7:
OLD EXCHANGE BUILDING

122 East Bay Street

 From Broad Street, cross East Bay Street to reach the Old Exchange Building.

Built between 1767 and 1771, this structure was renovated in 1818. It served as a post office during the war, but heavy Union shelling almost destroyed the building. The United States considered demolishing it because of the damage, but Charlestonians were able to preserve it after the war.[21]

Near Left:
The Old Exchange Building was a post office during the war, circa 1865. *Courtesy of the Library of Congress.*

Far Left:
The Old Exchange Building was heavily damaged during the Union bombardment of the Lower Peninsula.

STOP 8:
INGLIS ARCH HOUSE

91 East Bay Street

Turn right onto East Bay Street and continue walking towards White Point Garden. The Inglis Arch house will be on the right side.

Constructed between 1778 and 1782, this home was named for the old covered alley that runs through the first level. Also, a previous owner, George Inglis, had a store here. The home was damaged during the Union shelling of Charleston in 1864.[22]

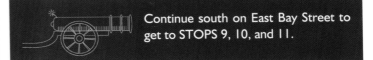
Continue south on East Bay Street to get to STOPS 9, 10, and 11.

STOP 9:
CASPER CHRISTIAN SCHUTT HOUSE

51 East Bay Street

Built by Casper Schutt, a wealthy German merchant, in 1799, subsequent owner John Fraser purchased it in 1821 and owned the home during the war. Fraser was the owner of Fraser & Company, which was involved in blockade running.

The owner of Fraser & Company, a blockade running business, John Fraser also owned this house.

STOP 10:
GENERAL WILMOT G. DESAUSSURE HOME

45 East Bay Street

Wilmot DeSaussure was born July 23, 1822; a Charleston lawyer and member of the South Carolina Legislature from 1848 to 1864, he constructed this home in 1852.

He commanded Fort Moultrie as a Lieutenant Colonel of the 1st Artillery Regiment of the South Carolina Militia after the Union's evacuation to Fort Sumter in December 1860. In April 1861, he commanded the Confederate artillery on Morris Island during the bombardment of Fort Sumter and later commanded a brigade of South Carolina militia and a division of reserves.

After the evacuation of Charleston in February 1865, his command joined Johnston's Army of Tennessee, surrendering at Durham, North Carolina, in April 1865. DeSaussure died in Florida in 1886 and is buried at Magnolia Cemetery.[23]

Confederate General Wilmot G. DeSaussure constructed this residence.

STOP 11:
PORCHER-SIMONDS HOME

29 East Battery

Francis Porcher, a Charleston cotton broker and a delegate to the South Carolina Secession Convention, constructed this home in 1856. He helped draft the Ordinance of Secession on December 20, 1860.

STOP 12:
NATHANIEL INGRAHAM HOUSE

2 Water Street

From East Bay Street, turn right onto Water Street.

Nathaniel Ingraham, a veteran of the Revolutionary War, built this home in 1818; it was later purchased by Otis Mills, owner of the Mills House Hotel. The home was damaged by Union shelling in 1864.

After the war, the home was bought by Dr. Edward Wells, a former Confederate soldier who wrote books about the Confederate infantry and two biographies about Wade Hampton.[24]

For "Stops 13 to 16," return to East Bay Street and walk South.

STOP 13:
EDMONDSTON-ALSTON HOUSE

21 East Battery

"The clustering shells illuminated the sky above it, hail upon Sumter's side. The first great scene of the opening drama of this momentous history."

~ *Charleston Courier*, April 12, 1861[25]

General Beauregard observed the bombardment of Fort Sumter from this piazza on April 12, 1861.

Completed in 1825, the Edmondston-Alston House suffered some damage from the war.

Shown is the East Battery as it appeared in 1865 during the Federal occupation. *Courtesy of the Library of Congress.*

In 1820, Charleston merchant Charles Edmondston began to construct this home, which was completed in 1825. Edmondston, in an effort to survive a nationwide financial panic, was forced to sell his home in 1838 and Charles Alston, a rice planter from Georgetown, South Carolina, purchased it. Alston renovated it to conform to Greek Revival, adding a third floor piazza, and altered the roofline by adding a parapet with the Alston coat of arms as his décor.

On April 12, 1861, General Beauregard and his staff watched the bombardment of Fort Sumter from the piazzas. The home offered a spectacular view of the Charleston Harbor and Fort Sumter. Seven months later, General Robert E. Lee spent a December evening here during the Charleston fire of 1861.

General Robert E. Lee was harbored here when the Mills House Hotel caught fire in December 1861. *Courtesy of the National Archives.*

Alston commanded Confederate forces on John's Island near the Stono River. These troops were located near a vacant plantation home. The *USS Isaac P. Smith* used the home for target practice, painting a figure on the house to add to their amusement. One day, Confederate troops occupied the house and captured the unsuspecting Union gunboat, renaming it the *CSS Stono*.[26]

In 1863, Alston's son, John Pringle, lost his life to typhoid fever while serving as lieutenant at Fort Sumter. He was twenty-seven years old.

The home was not damaged by Union shelling, but suffered some damage from a gun that was destroyed during the Confederate evacuation in February 1865.

Union General, Rufus Saxton, headquartered in nearby Beaufort, occupied the home after the Confederates.

STOP 14:
WILLIAM RAVENEL HOME

13 East Battery

"The live long night I tossed about — at half past four we hear the booming of the cannon — I start up, dress, and rush to my sisters. In misery we go on the housetop and see the shells bursting. They say our men are wasting ammunition."

~ Mary Boykin Chestnut, on the bombardment of Fort Sumter, April 12, 1861[27]

This home was built in 1845. Ravenel owned a cotton-exporting firm in Charleston. On April 12, 1861, spectators sat on this rooftop to watch the bombardment of Fort Sumter. Later, constant Union shelling of the Peninsula forced people to take refuge here.[28]

The William Ravenel Home was built in 1845... Charlestonians sat on its roof to watch the firing on Fort Sumter.

STOP 15: WILLIAM ROPER HOUSE

9 East Battery

Robert William Roper built this home in 1838. During the Confederate evacuation of Charleston in February 1865, soldiers destroyed and spiked artillery that had protected the Charleston Harbor. A barrel from one of these artillery pieces was destroyed, but a large part of the barrel landed in this home's attic. It was one of the largest Confederate guns and is still in the attic today.[29]

This home was damaged during the Confederate evacuation in February of 1865.

STOP 16:
JOHN RAVENEL HOME

5 East Battery

"Perhaps, I was mistaken, but it did occur to me that if we had then, instead of only one; just ten or twelve torpedoes to make a simultaneous attack on all the ironclads and this quickly followed by the equess of our rams, not only might this great fleet be destroyed, but the 10,000 troops on Morris Island been left at our mercy."

~ Lt. William I. Glassell, of the *CSS David*, on realizing that additional torpedo boats could have broken the Union's grasp around Charleston on October 5, 1863[30]

This home was constructed in 1848 by Dr. John Ravenal.

Dr. St. Julien Ravenal, John's son, invented the torpedo boat 'Little David.' It was fifty feet long, five feet in diameter, and cigar shaped. Steam driven, the boat was designed to break the Union blockade around Charleston. One of these vessels damaged the *USS New Ironsides* in October 1863, but rushing waters put out the fires that were ignited in the boiler room. The 'Little David' crew had to abandon ship; four crewmen escaped, but two were captured by the Union navy.

The Confederacy was short on materials, so a fleet of these torpedo boats was never fully constructed. Six of these vessels were found incomplete when Confederate forces evacuated Charleston on February 18, 1865. The technology was improvised and was used by the *Hunley* in its attack on the *Housatonic* in February 1864.[31]

Dr. St. Julien Ravenal invented the torpedo boats known as the *Little Davids*; one can be seen in the foreground.
Courtesy of the Library of Congress.

Chapter Four:

THE CHURCHES OF CHARLESTON

Walk back to White Point Garden and, from the Waterfront Park, cross over Bay Street onto Queen Street. Turn left onto State Street and then turn right onto Chalmers Street for STOPS 1 and 2.

The Cathedral of St. John the Baptist was burned in the Great Fire of December 1861.
Courtesy of the Library of Congress.

STOP 1:
OLD SLAVE MART

6 Chalmers Street
843-958-6467

This structure was built in 1859, as the city attempted to centralize and regulate the sale of slaves. It was decided that this location would be best utilized in the auctioning of slaves.[32] The mart was owned by John Ryan, who also sold, among other items, horses and stocks. Three years earlier, a city ordinance prohibited the sale of slaves in public, so this structure was constructed. It was turned into a museum in 1938, celebrating African history.

In 1859, the city of Charleston regulated the sale of slaves to certain locations.

STOP 2:
BIBLE DEPOSITORY

29 Chalmers Street

The Bible Depository was built in 1828. During the war, they raised money for Confederate troops.

STOP 3:
MILLS HOUSE HOTEL

115 Meeting Street

Continue walking west on Chalmers Street and turn right onto Meeting Street.

"General Lee is here, visiting the defenses. He is never hopeful and does not seem in particular good humor concerning things here. It seems to me there is miserable confusion, ignorance and inefficiency in every department."

~ From Mary Boykin Chesnut's Diary, November 14, 1861[33]

The Mills House Hotel as it appears today... It was restored in 1968.

Built in 1854, many delegates who attended the Democratic Convention in May 1860 were guests at this hotel.

In April 1861, spectators sat/stood on the rooftop to observe the bombardment of Fort Sumter.

In December 1861, General Robert E. Lee stood on a balcony of the hotel and watched the Great Fire that caused massive damage to the city before being moved to safety. By then, the fire had spread to the hotel, causing some damage.

General Beauregard had his headquarters here before moving to a home at 37 Meeting Street.

The hotel was restored in 1968.

The Mills House Hotel was damaged by fire in December 1861.
Courtesy of the Library of Congress.

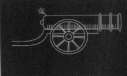

Continuing up Meeting Street, turn left onto Queen Street and then make another left onto King Street. Follow King until it intersects with Broad Street. Turn right, going west for STOPS 4 to 7.

STOP 4:
BEAUREGARD'S HEADQUARTERS

114 Broad Street

This home was the headquarters of General Beauregard from August to December of 1863.
President Jefferson Davis visited here in November after touring the Army of Tennessee near Chattanooga.

STOP 5:
CATHEDRAL OF
ST. JOHN THE BAPTIST

122 Broad Street

The original church was destroyed by the Great Fire of December 1861. Many people had thought the church had been fireproof and placed personal belongings here for safekeeping, which turned out to be a mistake.

The Catholic Diocese supported the Confederacy. Bishop Patrick Lynch traveled to the Vatican to seek papal recognition of the new government, but the Pope refused to give it. The Church was rebuilt in 1907.

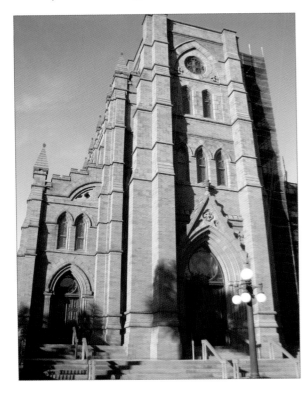

The Cathedral of St. John the Baptist was totally rebuilt in 1907.

STOP 6:
VALK HOUSE

125 Broad Street

Charles R. Valk owned this home during the war; he fought for the Confederacy.

STOP 7:
ALFRED HUGER HOME

140 Broad Street

Alfred Huger, Postmaster of the Confederacy, owned this home. Before the war, he was the local postmaster and the Postmaster of the Republic after the state's secession. After the war, he refused to sign the "iron clad oath" denouncing the Confederacy.

This home was rebuilt after the first house on the site burned in the Great Fire of December 1861.

STOP 8:
ST. JOHN'S
LUTHERAN CHURCH

10 Archdale Street

 Continue walking west on Broad Street until you get to Logan Street and then turn right. Walk up Logan Street and turn right onto Queen Street. Then turn left onto Archdale Street.

Dr. John Bachman was the pastor here from 1815 to 1874. He was a Union man, but he made the opening prayer at the Secession Convention. However, his support of the Union did not keep the church from being damaged by Union shelling during the war.

Church records and valuables were sent to Columbia for safekeeping during the war, but they were lost in Columbia's fire of February 1865.

STOP 9:
OLD JAIL

21 Magazine Street

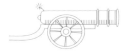 Continuing up Archdale Street, turn left onto Magazine Street.

"A dirty filthy place...unfit for human beings to live in."

~ An imprisoned Yankee officer, August 1864[34]

Built in 1802, the jail was damaged during the earthquake of 1886, but during the war soldiers from the 54th Massachusetts who had been captured at Battery Wagner were held here for eighteen months. Later they were sent to a Prisoner of War camp in Florence when Charleston was evacuated.

In the summer of 1864, more Union POWs were placed here when Sherman's army was approaching the POW camp at Andersonville, Georgia. Most of the prisoners were imprisoned inside the jail, but others were placed outside in tents — under the rifles of sentries on a forty-foot tower. Almost six hundred prisoners in total had been placed here.[35]

Soon Yellow Fever broke out; all of the sick prisoners were transported back to Andersonville while the rest of the prisoners were dispersed to other locations throughout South Carolina.

Union prisoners of war were held at this jail in 1864.

STOP 10:
JACOB FRANCIS HOUSE

25 Archdale Street

 Returning to Archdale Street, turn left. The house will be on your left.

Jacob Francis arrived in Charleston from Austria in 1858. When the war broke out, he became a blockade-runner. He built this house in 1886 and died here in 1903.

Jacob Francis, a former blockade-runner, built this home in 1886.

STOP 11:
CIRCULAR CONGREGATIONAL CHURCH

150 Meeting Street

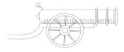 Continuing up Archdale Street, turn right onto Market Street. Keep on Market Street until you get to Meeting Street and turn right. You are now walking south.

The churchyard contains the grave of David Ramsay, who commanded the Union Light Infantry (Scottish) of the 17th Regiment in 1860; he captured the U.S. Arsenal on December 30, 1860.[36] Ramsay later commanded a company of the newly formed Charleston Battalion in February 1862, and was deployed on James Island in April 1862.

Initially, Ramsay was stationed at Secessionville and was promoted to Major within a few months.[37] He was present during the Union assault against Battery Wagner in July 1863 and was mortally wounded while leading a counterattack against the southeast salient; he was struck in the back by friendly fire during the confusion.[38] Ramsay was taken to his home, where he died August 4, 1863.[39]

The original church was destroyed by the Great Fire of December 1861 and rebuilt in 1892.

 Continuing down Meeting Street, turn right onto Queen Street and then turn left onto Church Street for STOPS 12 and 13.

STOP 12: FRENCH PROTESTANT CHURCH

140 Church Street

Built between 1844 and 1845, this church suffered heavy damage from Union shelling in 1864.[40]

STOP 13:
ST. PHILIP'S
EPISCOPAL CHURCH

147 Church Street

"As soon as the surrender was announced, the bells commenced ringing."
~ Charleston citizen, Emma Holmes, witnessed the bombardment
and surrender of Fort Sumter, April 12-13, 1861[41]

The present building was constructed between 1835 and 1838 after a fire in 1835.[42]

The bells were donated to the Confederacy and melted into munitions. The steeple was used as an observation post and was hit by Union shelling. The steeple was then painted black, so it could not be used as a point of reference for Union artillery.

A plaque commemorates church members who were killed while fighting for the Confederacy, and Confederate Colonel Cornelius Walker is buried in the churchyard.

Reverend Alexander Marshall refused to give the Episcopal prayer for Abraham Lincoln during the Union Occupation, so he was banished by Union General John Hatch and his property was confiscated. He returned after the hostilities ended.[43]

The church has two cemeteries; John C. Calhoun, who drafted the 1832 Nullification Papers advocating states' rights, was buried in one of them. When Sherman's troops approached Charleston, Calhoun's body was exhumed to an unmarked grave. It was reburied here after the war.

John C. Calhoun's body was exhumed and hidden from Yankee soldiers in early 1865.

The steeple was painted black during the war, so it could not be used as a reference point by Union artillery.

STOP 14:
POWDER MAGAZINE

79 Cumberland Street
843-722-9350
www.powdermag.org

 Continuing up Church Street, make a left onto Cumberland Street.

Constructed in 1713, it is one of the oldest buildings still in existence from before the American Revolution. It was used as a magazine until 1770. During the Civil War, it was used as a wine cellar.

The powder magazine served as a private wine cellar during the war.

STOP 15:
UNITED STATES CUSTOM HOUSE

200 East Bay Street

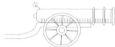 Turn around on Cumberland Street — going in the opposite direction of the previous Stop — you are now walking towards Bay Street.

Construction was begun before the war. A stonecutter, Alexander Campbell, was employed here until South Carolina seceded. Campbell returned with a Union invasion force on nearby James Island in June 1862.

The building was not fully completed until after the seizure of hostilities. Currently, it's the largest stone building in Charleston; the central great hall is open to the public Monday through Friday.

The Customs House was seized by South Carolina state forces in December 1860.

Chapter Five

THE MARKET

A view of The Market after Charleston was evacuated in February 1865. *Courtesy of the Library of Congress.*

STOP 1:
CONFEDERATE MUSEUM/MARKET

188 Meeting Street
843-723-1541
www.csa-scla.org

Construction began in 1788, but the building was not completed until sixteen years later. The lower level was used to sell vegetables, meats, and other goods. The second floor was built in 1841 and is now the Confederate Museum with many items on display, including banners that flew over Fort Sumter.

The second floor of the Market is now the home of a Confederate Museum.

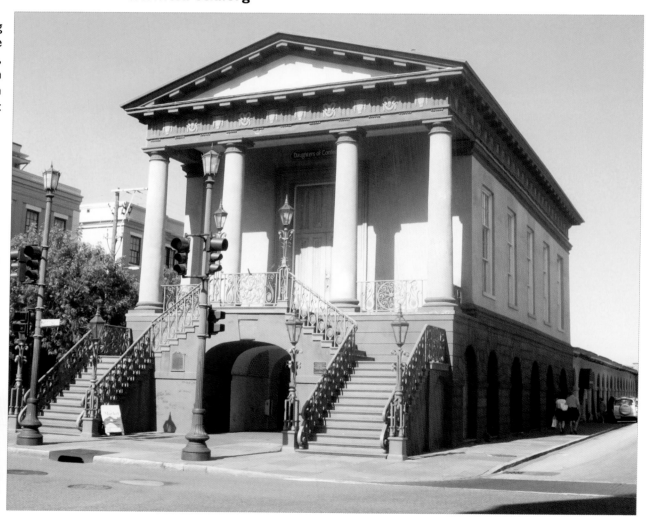

 Turn left onto Meeting Street and then turn right onto Pinckney Street. Continue on Pinckney Street until you get to Anson Street. Turn left for STOPS 2 and 3.

STOP 2:
COTTON WAREHOUSE

28 Anson Street

This building was a cotton warehouse during the war.

"George Williams who by order of the mayor of the city was on his way to meet US authorities and tender the surrender of Charleston."

~ George W. Williams, who was stopped by Federal probes outside the city[44]

Millionaire George W. Williams owned this warehouse. Cotton was either brought in through the railroads or the rivers; it was then purchased and sent to New York City.

As a Charleston alderman, Williams was responsible for contacting Union forces that Charleston had been evacuated in February 1865.

STOP 3:
EDWARD MCCRADY HOME

30 Anson Street

Edward McCrady built this home in 1838. Before the war, McCrady was a United States District Attorney in Charleston and a state legislator.

In 1863, McCrady defended captured African-American soldiers of the 54th Massachusetts Infantry after their failed assault on Battery Wagner. Through his arguments, they were spared execution because they were not runaway slaves or free Blacks, but were soldiers.

McCrady's son was also a lawyer and served with the Army of Northern Virginia, but he was severely wounded at Second Manassas and was discharged in January 1863.[45]

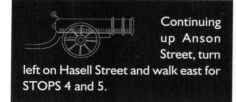

Continuing up Anson Street, turn left on Hasell Street and walk east for STOPS 4 and 5.

STOP 4:
WADE HAMPTON BIRTHPLACE

54 Hasell Street

Confederate General Wade Hampton was born at this home on March 28, 1818.

STOP 5: CONGREGATION BETH ELOHM

90 Hasell Street

This is the second oldest synagogue in the United States. The chandelier and organ were sent to Columbia for safekeeping during the war, but were lost when Columbia burned in 1865.

The synagogue was built in 1824.

Continuing down Hasell Street, turn right onto King Street. Continue north on King until you reach Society Street. Turn right and go east for STOPS 6 and 7.

STOP 6: ST. PAUL'S CATHOLIC CHURCH

63 Society Street

An active house of worship during the war, this former church is now a private residence.

STOP 7:
PHOEBE YATES PEMBER HOUSE

28 Society Street
843-722-4168
www.phoebepemberhome.com

"No one slept during the night of horror — for added to present scenes were the anticipations of what morrow would bring forth. Daylight dawned upon a wreck of destruction and desolation."

~ Phoebe Yates Pember evacuating Richmond, April 2, 1865[46]

Phoebe Yates Pember was born here in August 1823 and later moved to Savannah. She married in 1861, but lost her husband early in the war to disease.

In December 1862, she was appointed Chief Matron of a division at Chimborazo Hospital in Richmond — this hospital was the most productive of the entire war.

After the war, Pember returned to Savannah for a brief time before relocating to Baltimore, where she penned her memoirs in 1879, *A Southern Woman's Story*, which was an account of her service as a nurse.

Pember died in 1913 while visiting a friend in Savannah and is buried in Laurel Grove Cemetery. In 1995, the United States' Postal Service issued a series of stamps depicting events and people from the Civil War; Phoebe Yates Pember was on one of those stamps.[47]

The Pember house is now a Bed and Breakfast.

Turning around on Society Street so you're going in the opposite direction, follow it until you reach Meeting Street and turn right for STOPS 8 and 9.

Confederate Nurse Phoebe Yates Pember was born at this home in August of 1823.

STOP 8:
TRINITY UNITED METHODIST CHURCH

273 Meeting Street

This church was founded in 1791, but was burned and rebuilt in 1838. Confederate General Ellison Capers is buried in the churchyard.

STOP 9:
SOUTH CAROLINA SEA GRANT CONSORTIUM

287 Meeting Street

This building was used for organized meetings of the Washington Light Infantry, whose history dates back to 1807. They were organized into the First Regiment of Rifles in 1860 under the command of J. Johnston Pettigrew.[48] On December 27, 1860 they were part of a detachment that forcibly seized Castle Pinckney.[49]

In July 1861, the unit was ordered to stay and protect Charleston while sister companies participated in the Battle of First Manassas. Later that month, they were the honor guard for the body of General Barnard Bee, who fell at First Manassas.[50]

In July 1862, the Washington Light Infantry was organized into the 25th South Carolina Infantry; earlier members had opted to join Hampton's Legion at the start of the war.[51] They were positioned on James Island in July 1863 under the command of Colonel Charles H. Simonton[52] and were evacuated from Morris Island on September 6, 1863, along with the 27th and 28th Georgia regiments.[53]

During the winter of 1863-64, they were then reassigned to Hagood's Brigade and were sent to Virginia to help protect the Petersburg area and Drewery's Bluff. By the end of 1864, they had been sent south to Wilmington, North Carolina, and fought at the Second Battle of Fort Fisher in January 1865 — most of the regiment was lost here. The three companies that made up the Washington Light Infantry suffered more than twenty-five percent in casualties during the war.

This structure was used for organized meetings for members of the Washington Light Infantry both before and after the war.

STOP 10:
ST. JOHN'S REFORMED EPISCOPAL CHURCH

93 Anson Street

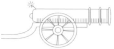

Continuing up Meeting Street, turn right onto George Street. Follow George Street until you reach Anson Street and turn left.

Built in 1850, this house of worship was originally owned by the Zion Presbyterian Church or the Anson Street Mission. Slaves were taught to read the Bible at this location before the war. In 1861, it became St. Joseph's Catholic Church and was known as "the Church of the Irish."

STOP 11:
ST. STEPHEN'S CHURCH

67 Anson Street

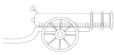

Turn around so you're going in the opposite direction. Walk down Anson Street and cross George Street.

This church was damaged by Union artillery during the war.

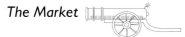

STOP 12:
C. D. FRANKE
COMPANY

38 Wentworth Street

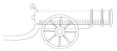 Continue walking down Anson Street and turn right onto Wentworth Street.

This company built gun carriages for the Confederacy.

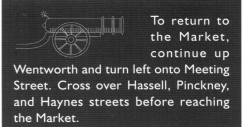

To return to the Market, continue up Wentworth and turn left onto Meeting Street. Cross over Hassell, Pinckney, and Haynes streets before reaching the Market.

Chapter Six:

CHARLESTON'S PATRIOTS

These munitions were captured by Union forces in February 1865. *Courtesy of the Library of Congress.*

STOP 1:
SEBRIG-AIMAR HOUSE

268 Calhoun Street

Start this walking tour from the west side of Cannon Park at Ashley Avenue. Once you get to Ashley Avenue, cross the street and turn right — you are walking north. Turn left onto Calhoun Street.

This home was occupied — and looted — by Federal troops in February 1865.

STOP 2: BEAUREGARD'S FINAL HEADQUARTERS

192 Ashley Avenue

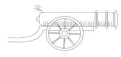

Return to Ashley Avenue and turn left. Walking north to Doughty Street, cross Ashley Avenue and continue walking northward.

General Beauregard had to move his headquarters here to escape the Union shelling on the Peninsula. In April 1864, he was transferred to command the Department of North Carolina and Southeastern Virginia.

This home served as Beauregard's final headquarters (December 1863-April 1864) before he was transferred to Virginia in 1864.

STOP 3: COLONEL ALFRED RHETT'S HOUSE

109 Cannon Street

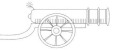

Continue walking up Ashley Avenue and turn right onto Cannon Street. Stop at the corner.

Alfred Rhett was the son of secessionist Robert Barnwell Rhett. During the ironclad attack on Fort Sumter in April 1863, the garrison was under Alfred's command. He later killed another officer in a duel over a questionable promotion, but Rhett called the killing self-defense.

Rhett later commanded troops in the city of Charleston and evacuated the city in February 1865. On March 15, 1865, he was captured at the Battle of Averasboro in North Carolina, after mistakenly coming under the care of Union cavalry scouts.

After the war, Rhett served as Charleston's Chief of Police, but died of malaria that he had contracted on his Ogeechee River plantation near Savannah.

This home was owned by Colonel Alfred Rhett, who was later captured at the Battle of Averasboro, North Carolina, in March 1865.

STOP 4:
ASHLEY HALL
(George Alfred Trenholm Home)

172 Rutledge Avenue

Facing the Rhett House, turn left onto Cannon Street and walk in an eastwardly direction. Turn right onto Rutledge Avenue and continue south. Cross over Bee Street and stop before crossing Doughty Street.

"The parlors were all very grand and the sofas luxurious."

~ 15-year-old Midshipman James Morris Morgan, who was stationed in Charleston in August 1862, later married one of Trenholm's daughters.[54]

George Alfred Trenholm was born in Charleston February 25, 1807. He soon became a well-respected banker and businessman after leaving school in 1823. Trenholm went to work for John Fraser & Company, Charleston's leading cotton exporter. In 1853, he was put at the firm's head, as chief owner; other financial holdings included steamships, railroads, banks, hotels, plantations, wharves, and cotton presses.

Between 1852 and 1853, Trenholm served in the South Carolina Legislature and was a strong advocate for secession. When war broke out in 1861, he offered his business skills and resources to the Confederacy.

Trenholm opened a branch of Fraser, Trenholm & Company in Liverpool, England. This branch operated as the South's financial agent, employing sixty ships that ran the Federal blockade. Additional offices were opened in Nassau and Bermuda. His company shipped out cotton, tobacco, and turpentine and returned with coal, iron, salt, ammunition, and arms, including the South's first 40,000 Enfield rifles that were purchased in Britain.

By 1863, it was estimated that Trenholm had earned $9 million in running the blockade. During his tenure, he initially served as an advisor to Confederate

This home is now a private girl's school.

Treasury Secretary Christopher Memminger and later became the head of that department in July 1864. He tried many last-ditch efforts to earn more money for the Confederacy, but the Confederate Congress blocked his efforts. He was captured in April 1865 and held prisoner at Fort Pulaski until October 1865.

After the war, he returned to Charleston, but was bankrupt. Trenholm reorganized his company and by 1868 had regained his fortune. He also served again in the legislature from 1874 to 1876, until he passed away. He is buried at Magnolia Cemetery. It is thought by many scholars that Margaret Mitchell based her character Rhett Butler from *Gone with the Wind* on Trenholm.

STOP 5:
ROBERT BARNWELL RHETT, SR. HOME

6 Thomas Street

Continue walking south on Rutledge Avenue and turn left at the next stoplight, onto Vanderhorst Street. Continue on Vanderhorst until you reach Thomas Street and turn left.

Before the war, this was the home of Robert Barnwell Rhett, Sr. He owned the *Charleston Mercury* newspaper and used it to promote his views on states' rights and slavery. He had served in Congress and was a political ally of John C. Calhoun. After Calhoun died, he represented South Carolina in the senate. He resigned in 1852, when South Carolina refused to secede over California, and in December 1860, delivered a speech urging other cotton states to leave the Union after South Carolina claimed her independence.

Note: In 1850, California was originally designated to enter the Union as two states, Lower California and Upper California. Lower California as a slave state, but residents rejected that idea and California entered the Union as a free state under The Great Compromise.

This home was owned by Robert B. Rhett Sr., a political ally of John C. Calhoun, and later sold to Blockade Runner George Trenholm during the war.

STOP 6:
EDWARD TRENHOLM HOME

91/93 Rutledge Avenue

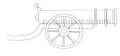

Returning to Vanderhorst Street, turn right. When you get to Smith Street, turn left. Continue on Smith Street, crossing Calhoun and Bull streets, and turn right onto Montagu Street. Cross Rutledge Avenue.

Edward Trenholm, George's brother, owned this home. He was also a blockade-runner.

STOP 7:
WILLIAM LAUGHTON HOME

101 Rutledge Avenue

Turn right onto Rutledge and continue walking to the next corner.

William Laughton was a Charleston cotton and rice merchant from Great Britain. During the war, he fought for the South.

STOP 8:
BEE RANGE

101-109 Bull Street

 From the Laughton home, turn left at the next cross street, Bull Street.

"Poor Jamie Bee was the first whose death was announced, but Yankee Prisoners taken today say he is not dead, but desperately wounded."

~ Childhood friend Emma Holmes on hearing the initial reports of the fighting at Battery Wagner, July 11, 1863[55]

William C. Bee, the owner of a blockade-running company, owned these homes. The homes were used to store and sell the merchandise that was brought in through the Federal blockade.

William Bee lost two sons during the war: James Ladson Bee was wounded and captured at Morris Island; he later died in Union hands. His other son, John Stock Bee, was killed at the Battle of Cold Harbor in June 1864.

These homes were built between 1849 and 1854

STOP 9:
HAMILTON-BENNETT HOUSE

113 Ashley Avenue

 Continue on Bull Street. Turn right on Ashley Avenue.

Homeowner, Paul Hayne, served at Fort Sumter during the first year of the war. His tuberculosis forced him out of active duty. He then wrote about Stonewall Jackson and the defenses of Vicksburg and Charleston.

The home was shelled during the war and valuables were stolen by Union troops. He was broke after the war, after having invested in Confederate bonds. He later moved to Augusta, Georgia, where he died.

Vandalized by Union troops, this home was built in 1855.

 Continuing up Ashley Avenue, go to Cannon Park. Tour Ends.

Chapter Seven:
PRISONS AND HOSPITALS

Union officers were held as prisoners at this home during the summer of 1864. *Courtesy of the Library of Congress.*

STOP 1:
UNION PRISON

180 Broad Street

This home was owned by George W. Cooper before it was used as a prison for Yankee officers.

From the southern end of Colonial Lake Park, which runs parallel with Broad Street, turn right onto Broad Street and cross over Rutledge Avenue.

"For some time it has been known that a batch of Yankee prisoners, comprising the highest in rank now in our hands, were soon to be brought hither to share in the pleasures of the bombardment. These prisoners we understand will be furnished with comfortable quarters in that portion of the city most exposed to enemy fire. The commanding officer on Morris Island will be duly notified of the fact of their presence in the shelled district and if his batteries still continue at their wanton and barbarous work, it will be at the peril of the captive officers."

~ The *Charleston Mercury*, June 1864

Five Union generals were held prisoner at this house in an effort to stop Union shelling of the Lower Peninsula.

In the summer of 1864, the Confederates believed that if they scattered Union POWs throughout the Peninsula it would force the Yankees to abandon the bombarding of Charleston. The plan did not work. Union General Foster countered by placing six hundred Confederate prisoners in a stockade on Morris Island, which was under Confederate fire from Fort Sumter.

Later that autumn, the Union prisoners were sent inland and the Confederate prisoners were removed to Fort Pulaski.

STOP 2:
SAMUEL WRAGG SIMONS HOUSE

164 Broad Street

Continuing east on Broad Street, cross over Trapman Street to reach this site.

Samuel Wragg Simons was a Confederate soldier who served as a corporal with the Charleston Light Dragoons. The Dragoons were assigned to the Department of South Carolina, Georgia, and Florida, protecting the railroads around Charleston.

Simons and his unit were later consolidated with two cavalry battalions to form the 4th South Carolina Cavalry — the Dragoons became Company K — that continued to serve in the Charleston area until March 1864, when the regiment was transferred to Jeb Stuart's cavalry in Virginia. Simons participated in the Battles of the Wilderness, Spotsylvania, Cold Harbor, and the Siege of Petersburg. By the spring of 1865, they were dispatched to confront Sherman's invasion of North Carolina.

Simons surrendered with the Army of Tennessee on April 26, 1865. During the war, a fellow Confederate soldier had accidentally wounded him in the face in a case of friendly fire. After the war, Simons worked for a cotton exporting company, where he eventually became manager. He became financially successful and built two adjoining houses at 166 and 168 Broad Street.

This home was owned by Samuel Wragg Simons, who served with the Charleston Light Dragoons during the war.

STOP 3: ANOTHER GEORGE W. COOPER HOUSE

13 Franklin Street

 Continue east on Broad Street and turn left onto Franklin Street.

This was another Cooper-owned house during the war.

STOP 4: OLD MARINE HOSPITAL

20 Franklin Street

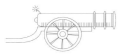 Continuing up Franklin Street, cross over Queen Street to get to this site.

Before the war broke out in 1861, this was a home for sick sailors. During the war, it was used as a Confederate Hospital. After the war, it was used as a free school for African-American children. It is now the Housing Authority for the City of Charleston.

The Old Marine Hospital was utilized as a Confederate infirmary during the war.

STOP 5: UNION PRISON

1 Pitt Street

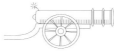 As you continue walking up Franklin Street, it will become Wilson Street. Continue until you reach Beaufain Street and turn left. Then turn right onto Pitt Street.

"We understand that the petticoat sympathizers with the Yankee prisoners were again busy in their shameful vocation, yesterday."

~ Clip from a Charleston newspaper after the attack on Battery Wagner[56]

This home also served as a Union prison.

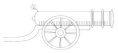

STOP 6:
DUNCAN N. INGRAHAM HOME

89 Beaufain Street

Return to Beaufain Street and turn right. The home will be on the left.

Duncan N. Ingraham served as a commodore in the Confederate Navy. *Courtesy of the National Archives.*

"I directed Lieutenant Rutledge to require Lieutenant Commander Abbot, of the damaged *USS Meredita*, his word of honor for his commander, officers and crew that they would not serve against the Confederate States until regularly exchanged."

~ Commodore Ingraham to his aide after the *USS Meredita* asked for terms of surrender, January 31, 1863[57]

Duncan Ingraham was born in Charleston December 6, 1802 and entered the Navy as a Midshipman at the age of ten. Much of his pre-Civil War duty was served in the Mediterranean.

Ingraham resigned his commission when South Carolina seceded in December 1860 and then commanded Confederate naval forces along the South Carolina coast from November 1861 to March 1863 as a Commodore. During his tenure, he oversaw the construction of ironclads; it was thought that a fleet of ironclads could break the Union naval blockade, but the South never had the resources to implement such an ironclad attack against the blockading naval squadrons around Charleston.

Age forced Ingraham away from sea duty in 1863 and he commanded the shore installations until Charleston fell in 1865. He died here October 16, 1891.

Built in 1816, Ingraham owned this home during the war.

Continuing on Beaufain Street, turn left onto Smith Street. Follow Smith Street until it intersects with Queen Street and turn left. Stay on Queen Street and then turn right onto Trapman Street. Make another right onto Broad Street — this will take you back to Colonial Lake Park.

TOURING CHARLESTON… BY CAR

This section will allow you to visit sites that were outside the city limits during the war.

Chapter Eight:

THE HUNLEY AND CHARLESTON CEMETERIES

Magnolia Cemetery's monument to her Confederate dead.

STOP 1:
CHARLESTON VISITORS CENTER

375 Meeting Street
843-724-7174
www.charlestoncvb.com

During the Civil War, this structure was used as a depot for the Charleston and Savannah Railroad. Supplies and troops were shuttled along this line, including all points between Charleston and Savannah. On November 2, 1863, Jefferson Davis arrived at the terminal from Savannah.

STOP 2:
THE HUNLEY
Warren Lesch Conservation Center

1250 Supply Street

From the Charleston Visitor's Center, turn left onto Meeting Street and drive 1.2 miles. Turn left onto Interstate 26 West and drive 2.2 miles to Exit 218 (Spruill Avenue and the Naval Base). Turn left onto Spruill Avenue and drive .8 miles to Naval Base Road. Turn right and travel .4 miles to Hobson Avenue. Follow the signs to the Warren Lesch Conservation Center.

"I am authorized to say that John Fraser and Company will pay over to any parties who shall destroy *USS New Ironsides* the sum of $100,000. A similar sum for the destruction of the wooden frigate *Wabash* and the sum of $50,000 for every monitor."

~ Thomas Jordan, Beauregard's Chief of Staff, putting a bounty on ships of the Federal Blockade in August 1863[58]

In 1862, Horace Hunley and two other inventors were forced to flee from Union naval forces around New Orleans; they had been working on the *Pioneer*, a submarine that had to be scuttled in Lake Pontchartrain. The team relocated to Alabama to continue their research.[59]

In Mobile, they had additional assistance from local machinists who helped construct a second submarine, the *American Diver*. It was ready by early 1863, but sea trials proved that it was too slow to present a real threat. It later sank during a thunderstorm.[60]

They immediately began work on their third project, the *H. L. Hunley*, using the information from the two previous projects. She passed her sea trials in Mobile Bay and was shipped to Charleston in hopes of breaking the Yankee blockade.

On August 23, 1863, during a test dive, human error caused the *Hunley* to sink with five lives lost, but she was recovered. Two months later, Horace Hunley and a crew of seven failed to resurface after a mock attack, but again the ship was recovered. The program was then transferred to the Confederate Army with volunteers who trained for the attack against the *Housatonic* that occurred on February 17, 1864.[61]

The *Hunley* was found on May 3, 1995, by best selling author Clive Cussler. It was found about four miles from Sullivan's Island. It was covered with silt, basically protecting it from erosion. On August 8, 2000, a harness was placed around the *Hunley* with floatation devices to bring it to the surface and she was placed on a barge and brought to the conservation center. Photographs of the submarine are prohibited, but for more information go to www.hunley.org.

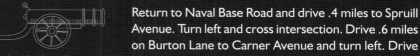

Return to Naval Base Road and drive .4 miles to Spruill Avenue. Turn left and cross intersection. Drive .6 miles on Burton Lane to Carner Avenue and turn left. Drive 2.4 miles — Carner Avenue will merge into Meeting Street Road. Turn left onto Cunnington Avenue and follow to the three cemeteries (STOPS 3, 4, and 5).

STOP 3:
MAGNOLIA CEMETERY

70 Cunnington Avenue

Brigadier General James Conner (1829-1883)

"There is no question, but that General Connor was of the best officers that South Carolina furnished during the war."

~ Captain D. Augustus Dickert served with Conner in the Shenandoah Valley in 1864[62]

James Conner was born in Charleston in 1829; in 1849, he graduated from South Carolina College. He was admitted to the bar in 1852, practicing law in Charleston. In 1856, Conner was appointed District Attorney, but resigned in December 1860. Initially, when the war broke out he was appointed Confederate States District Attorney for South Carolina, but he declined the position.

Connor volunteered as captain of the Washington Light Infantry in May 1861, serving with the Army of Northern Virginia until October 1864. Conner participated in most of the campaigns and lost a leg at the Battle of Cedar Run on October 12, 1864.

After the war, Conner returned to his law practice and was elected Attorney General in 1876. Conner died in Richmond in 1883; his remains were returned to Charleston.

Brigadier General Micah Jenkins (1835-1864)

"I am happy; I have felt despair of the cause for some months, but am relieved, and feel assured we will put the enemy back across the Rapidan before night."

~ Jenkins, confident of victory, riding with Gen. Longstreet before he was mortally wounded at the Battle of the Wilderness, May 6, 1864[63]

Micah Jenkins was born into a cotton planter's family on Edisto Island in 1835. He graduated from the Citadel in 1851 and later helped establish Kings Mountain Military School. When the war broke out, he helped organize the 5th South Carolina Infantry and was elected its colonel.

Jenkins fought at First Manassas and the Peninsula Campaign. In July 1862, Jenkins was promoted to Brigadier General and was wounded while leading his brigade at Second Manassas.

He rejoined the army at Fredericksburg, serving in every campaign with the First Corps, except Gettysburg and Chickamauga. Jenkins rejoined the corps after the Battle of Chickamauga and served until he was mortally wounded by his own men at the Battle of the Wilderness on May 6, 1864.

Brigadier General Sabine Ripley (1823-1887)

Sabine Ripley was born in Worthington, Ohio, March 14, 1823 and graduated from West Point in 1843. During the Mexican War, he was noted for gallantry. He married one of the Middletons of Charleston in 1852 and resigned his commission a year later.

For the next seven years, Ripley was a prominent businessman and was appointed a colonel of South Carolina forces in 1860. Ripley led the force into Fort Moultrie after U.S. troops evacuated it on December 26 and again at Fort Sumter after it fell in April 1861.

In August 1861, Ripley was appointed Brigadier General and joined the Army of Northern Virginia, fighting with the army from the Peninsula to Sharpsburg, where he was wounded. A year later he returned to active duty in Charleston and joined the Army of Tennessee after the evacuation of Charleston in February 1865.

Magnolia's Confederate dead are still honored.

This is the final resting place for three *Hunley* crewmembers.

After the war, Ripley was in Great Britain trying to establish a manufacturing firm there that later failed. He returned to Charleston and died in New York City on March 29, 1887, but was laid to rest in Charleston.[64]

H. L. *Hunley* Memorial

This plot is where all three crews of the *Hunley* are buried. The final crew was laid to rest April 17, 2004 after a four and a half-hour procession that marched from downtown Charleston to the cemetery.

Charleston Light Dragoons

Formed in 1792, during the Civil War the unit initially served along the coast, protecting the railroad lines. The unit was composed of Charleston's most prestigious families. In 1864, the Dragoons consolidated into the 4th South Carolina Cavalry, Company K. They were soon transferred to Virginia and finished off the war in North Carolina, trying to slow Sherman's advance in March 1865.

The Charleston Light Dragoons were composed of members from Charleston's most illustrious families.

STOP 4:
BETHANY CEMETERY

10 Cunnington Avenue

German Light Artillery Monument

The German Light Artillery was formed of Charlestonians of German heritage in December 1860 and soon occupied Fort Moultrie. The unit was expanded in August 1861 and the company was transferred to Virginia in September. They were initially assigned to Wade Hampton's Legion as Company B of Hampton's Legion Artillery (known as the German Light Artillery).

Under Lee's orders, the Army of Northern Virginia was reorganized and the German Light Artillery was assigned to General Longstreet's Corps, serving from the Peninsula to Gettysburg. After the fighting in Pennsylvania, they were redeployed near Pocotalico, protecting the Charleston and Savannah Railroad, and were later assigned to the Department of South Carolina, Georgia and Florida until the end of the war.

During Sherman's invasion of South Carolina, they assembled with the Army of Tennessee in March 1865 at Fayetteville, fighting at Averasboro and Bentonville. They were then ordered to Camden, South Carolina, but learned that the major Confederate armies had surrendered, so they disbanded and returned home without surrendering.

The German Light Artillery served in South Carolina and with the Army of Northern Virginia.

STOP 5:
ST. LAWRENCE CEMETERY

60 Huguenot Avenue

Irish Volunteers Monument

This monument honors the Charleston soldiers of Irish descent who served with the Confederate armies.

The 1st South Carolina Infantry, Company K, was organized in Richmond in August 1861. The regiment served with the Army of Northern Virginia from the Peninsula Campaign to Appomattox.

The Charleston Battalion, Company C, was formed in the spring of 1862 and was assigned to the Department of South Carolina, Georgia and Florida during 1862 and 1863. The battalion fought at Secessionville and Battery Wagner. In September 1863, the unit merged with others to form the 27th South Carolina Infantry, as Company H.

The newly formed 27th South Carolina Infantry initially served at Fort Sumter, but was reassigned to the Army of Northern Virginia in the spring of 1864. The regiment served from Cold Harbor to Petersburg. Later transferred to the Army of Tennessee, they surrendered at Durham, North Carolina, in April 1865.

To return to the Visitor's Center, return to Meeting Street Road, turn left, and drive 1.8 miles.

Chapter Nine:

MOUNT PLEASANT

This Confederate blockade-runner ran aground on Sullivan's Island. *Courtesy of the Library of Congress.*

STOP 1:
FORT MOULTRIE

1214 Middle Street

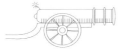 From the Visitor's Center, turn right onto Meeting Street and then turn left onto John Street. Turn left onto East Bay Street and drive .3 miles. Turn right onto US 17 North toward Mount Pleasant and drive 2.2 miles over the Ravenal Bridge. Exit right onto SC 703; stay in left lane. Drive on SC 703 (Coleman Boulevard) for 5 miles. Turn right onto Middle Street and drive .3 miles to Fort Moultrie.

"It was my solemn duty to move my command from a fort which we could not have held longer than forty-eight or sixty hours, to this one, where my power of resistance is increased to a very great degree."

~ Major Robert Anderson
in a report to Washington about his evacuation to Fort Sumter,
December 26, 1860

Fort Moultrie remained active until the end of the Second World War.

The first fort was built during the Revolutionary War and, while it was not completed when the British attacked on June 28, 1776, it was able to resist the assaults. The fort was named after its commander, Colonel William Moultrie, and was occupied by the British in 1780 after Charleston was overrun. Fort Moultrie was returned after the war.

After the Revolution, the fort was neglected and remained unchanged until 1794, when Congress authorized a coastal defensive system along the Atlantic Coast. The second fort was completed in 1798, but neglect and a hurricane destroyed it in 1804. Construction began on the third fort — the present fortification — in 1809.

By 1860, numerous improvements had been made; the armament had been updated and the parapet was altered. It was part of a ring of forts that circled Charleston Harbor while Fort Sumter guarded the entrance to the harbor.

On December 26, 1860, Major Robert Anderson and his garrison abandoned Fort Moultrie in favor of Fort Sumter. Anderson had been given this assignment in November 1860. Because he was a Southerner from Kentucky; Washington believed he would not provoke a war.

Anderson believed Moultrie could not be well defended because the fort was designed to defend against a naval intruder — not forces from downtown Charleston — so he moved to stronger protection at Fort Sumter. Before Anderson left, he spiked the guns, burned the gun carriages, and left much of his supply. The garrison marched out at nightfall to awaiting boats along the sea wall. South Carolina forces occupied the fort on the following day.

In February 1861, it was turned over to the Confederate States of America after the formation of the new government in Montgomery, and on April 12, 1861, Fort Moultrie participated in the 34-hour bombardment of Fort Sumter.

In April 1863, the Siege of Charleston had begun and lasted until February 17, 1865. Yankee ironclads and shore batteries fired on Moultrie for the next twenty months. The Confederates placed sand to help protect the walls, but the Union's rifled artillery had taken its toll on the masonry structure.

The fort was modernized in the 1870s, with the addition of new artillery, concrete magazines, and bomb proofs that were buried beneath the earth. The fort remained active until World War II.

Damage from Federal artillery. *Courtesy of the Library of Congress.*

Gun carriages burn at Fort Moultrie, as Charleston residents awaken.
Courtesy of Fort Sumter National Monument.

Fort Moultrie, circa 1865. *Courtesy of the Library of Congress.*

Guns from this section of Fort Moultrie fired on Fort Sumter in April 1861.

The present fortification was built in 1809

STOP 2:
BATTERY MARSHALL

Breach's Inlet

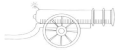

Exiting the parking lot of Fort Moultrie, turn left onto Middle Street and drive 3 miles. Pull off on the right and park in the lot.

"The Fish (the *Hunley*) went direct for her victim, and her torpedo striking the side, tore a tremendous hole in the *Housatonic*, which sank to the bottom in four minutes. The Fish was never seen again."

~ Private Arthur Ford,
of Buist's Battery of South Carolina Artillery,
at Breach's Inlet, February 17, 1864[65]

During the war, a Confederate fortification was placed here and, on the moonlit night of February 17, 1864, the *Hunley* passed through this point on its way to attack the *Housatonic*. It was thought that this crude submarine might break the tightening Union blockade around Charleston Harbor. They passed through here about 9 p.m.; she was armed with a harpoon torpedo. When she arrived with her crew, the *Housatonic* fired small arms at her. As she pulled away, Lieutenant Dixon ignited the 135-pound charge — the *Housatonic* sank in three minutes, but the *Hunley* never returned. The crew of the *Hunley* did signal observers that their mission had succeeded, but the ship sank and was not found until 1995.

Battery Marshall, circa 1865.
Courtesy of the Library of Congress.

Shown is Confederate artillery in action at Battery Marshall.

The *CSS Hunley* passed here on the night of February 17, 1864.

STOP 3:
BOONE HALL PLANTATION

1235 Long Point Road
843-884-4371
www.boonehallplantation.com

Exit the parking lot of Battery Marshall to the right. Turn right onto Jasper Boulevard. Drive 1.8 miles and turn left onto SC 517. Drive 3.8 miles to US 17 North and turn right. Drive 1 mile, move into the left lane, and at traffic light, turn left onto Long Point Road — Boone Hall is .7 miles on your right.

Slave quarters still dot the Boone Hall landscape.

Slaves prepare cotton before the war.
Courtesy of the Library of Congress.

The land around the plantation was granted in 1681 to Major John Boone, one of South Carolina's first settlers. In 1743, Boone's son planted the Live Oak Trees at the entrance of Boone Hall Plantation. It is not known when the house was built, but the property was subdivided in 1718 among Boone's children and remained in the Boone family until 1811, when it was purchased by John and Henry Horlbeck.

By 1850, Boone Hall was one of the leading cotton producing plantations around Charleston. It also produced bricks for the construction of Fort Sumter. During the war, earthworks were erected on the property to protect the northern perimeter of Charleston's defenses.

The property was sold in 1935 and the current house was constructed. The exterior of Boone Hall was filmed as the Mount Royal Plantation from the ABC mini-series "North & South."

To return to Charleston, turn left out of Boone Hall and drive .7 miles to US 17. Turn right onto 17 South and follow into downtown Charleston.

Several major motion picture companies have used Boone Hall for location shoots.

The first of these Live Oaks were planted in 1743.

Boone Hall's Avenue of Oaks.

Chapter Ten:

ASHLEY RIVER PLANTATIONS

A view of Drayton Hall from the Ashley River.

STOP 1:
WAYSIDE (1ST LOUISIANA) HOSPITAL

564 & 570 King Street

 As you leave the Visitor's Center, turn left onto Meeting Street and then make another left onto Mary Street. From Mary Street, turn right onto King Street.

This hospital was established in July 1862 — cases that could not be treated in field or regimental hospitals were sent here. Then, the soldiers were moved to other hospitals in Georgia and South Carolina when they were strong enough to travel. Additional room was leased at 570 King Street and,

by 1865, Wayside was one of only three hospitals still operating in Charleston, as most had been evacuated to other cities by this time.

Dr. Robert Lebby, Sr., a native of Charleston, was appointed a surgeon in the Confederate Army in December 1862 and was in command of the hospital until the end of the war.

The name of the hospital was changed to the 1st Louisiana Hospital in December 1863 so that soldiers could be sent to hospitals that were named for their home states.

STOP 2:
THE CITADEL MUSEUM

171 Moultrie Street
843-953-6846
www.citadel.edu

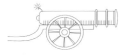 From Wayside Hospital, turn back onto King Street and drive about 1 mile. Turn left onto Moultrie Street and drive .6 miles.

The Citadel was founded in 1842; the cadets fired the opening shots of the Civil War when they fired on the *Star of the West* from Morris Island on January 9, 1861.

Cadets from the Citadel continued to aid the Confederate army by helping to drill recruits, manufacture ammunition, protect arms depots, and guard Union prisoners. The cadets also served in numerous engagements around the Charleston area. The school relocated to this site in 1922.

The museum has numerous Civil War exhibits.

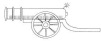

STOP 3:
DRAYTON HALL

3380 Ashley River Road
843-769-2600
www.draytonhall.org

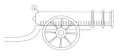 Departing the museum, turn right onto Elmwood Avenue and drive .2 miles. Turn right onto Congress Street and then make a quick left onto Hagood Avenue. Drive .6 miles to Spring Street. Turn right and go .2 miles. Take ram for US 17 South for .5 miles; get off at Exit 17 onto SC 61 and drive about 8 miles.

(Note: As you drive to Drayton Hall, you will pass Fort Bull at the intersection of Ashley River Road and Bee Ferry Road. It was constructed in 1863 to prevent a Union attack on the west side of Charleston. The British attacked this area in 1780 and captured the city. The fort was occupied until February 1865.)

Construction on Drayton Hall started in 1738 and was completed in 1742. The plantation grew rice and indigo. The home always remained in the possession of the Draytons, many of whom served the Confederate cause.

After the evacuation of Charleston, Union forces appeared on the grounds, but did not enter the home. Signs had been posted around the property that fever was present and the home was a hospital for the victims of the epidemic. The myth worked and the home was saved. It was later used as a command post for General Hatch.

It is thought that many slaves who escaped from Drayton Hall went to Hilton Head Island and joined Union forces there. They served in the 2nd Regiment of U.S. Colored Light Artillery and various Colored Infantry regiments.

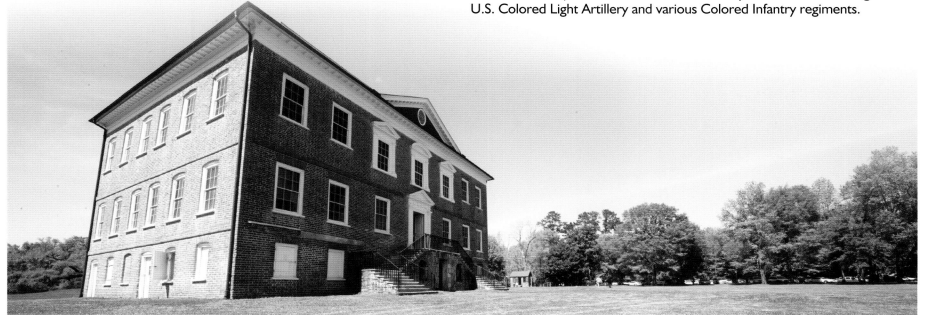

This sign, posted to warn about the presence of fever, prevented the house from being sacked by Union troops.

The rear view of Drayton Hall.

This plantation grew rice and indigo before the war.

Drayton Family Members

J. S. (James) Drayton, 1820-1867

James was mustered into service in Charleston in December 1861, as a member of Company B, 3rd Battalion, South Carolina Light Artillery, which was also known as the Palmetto Battalion.

James also served in the Department of Mississippi and East Louisiana and participated in the fighting around Jackson, Mississippi. He later served with the Army of Tennessee, from Atlanta to Sherman's campaigns into Georgia and the Carolinas.

The Battalion surrendered April 26, 1865, at Durham, North Carolina.

T. H. M. (Thomas) Drayton, 1828-1867

Tom was born in Charleston, but in the late 1840s he relocated to Brazoria County, Texas, where he established his own cotton plantation with his family's money. In 1861, he joined the 8th Texas Cavalry known as Terry's Texas Rangers, enlisting as a private.

Mustered into service in Houston, Tom served at Shiloh, Murfreesboro, Chickamauga, Atlanta, and Sherman's Campaign against Georgia and the Carolinas. He surrendered at Durham, North Carolina, in April 1865.

Dr. John Drayton, 1831-1912

John supervised Drayton Hall during the war. In June 1863, he was assigned Acting Medical Director of Laborers and Negroe Laborers for the Engineering Department on James Island. These laborers were used for constructing defensive works.

It is thought that he put up a sign indicating the presence of fever at Drayton Hall to keep Union troops from torching the house in February 1865. He moved to Texas after the war, raising cotton on his plantation, 'El Dorado.' He died in Mexico in 1912.

Charles Drayton, 1847-1915

Charles served with various units in the service of the Army of Northern Virginia.

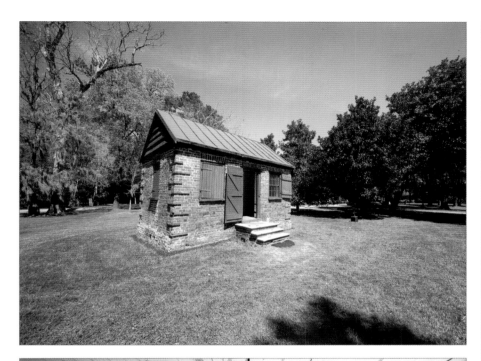

Drayton Hall's lone remaining slave cabin is now part of the **Drayton Hall** museum.

Four Drayton brothers fought for the Confederacy.

STOP 4:
MAGNOLIA PLANTATION & GARDENS

3350 Ashley River Road
843-571-1266
www.magnoliaplantation.com

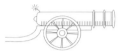 Leaving Drayton Hall, turn right onto SC 61 and drive .5 miles to Magnolia Plantation — the house will be on your right.

Founded in 1679 and cultivating rice, this is the oldest plantation on the Ashley River. The gardens were established late in the seventeenth century and continued to grow and expand until the nineteenth century. It was Mathew Brady, the most prominent photographer of the times, photographed these gardens before the Civil War.

During the war, the Reverend John Grimke Drayton owned the house; he adopted the surname because his aunts, Sarah and Angelina Grimke, were high profiled abolitionists. The long bridge was built in the 1840s. The main house was burned during the war, either by slaves or Union troops.

The current home was built just before the Revolutionary War; it was built in Summerville and transported down the Ashley River to this location in 1873. It had been a family summer residence.

After the Civil War, the gardens were opened for admission, which helped save the house from economic ruin in the 1870s.

Many creatures that call Magnolia home patrol these luscious grounds.

This was a family summer home that was built before the Revolution.

These gardens were established late in the seventeenth century and opened to the public in the early 1870s.

Dating back to 1679, Magnolia is the oldest plantation on the Ashley River.

Azaleas bloom in early April.

This plantation produced cotton and rice.

The bridges were erected in the 1840s.

The main Magnolia house was burned in 1865.

The gardens feature bamboo.

STOP 5:
MIDDLETON PLANTATION

4300 Ashley River Road
843-722-7171
www.middletonplace.org

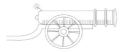 On exiting Magnolia Plantation, turn right onto SC 61 and drive 3.7 miles to the Middleton Plantation — it will be on your right.

"One of our foraging parties, under Captain Armstrong, met with Major Smith of the 56th New York and was ordered to burn Middleton home on Thursday, February 23, 1865."

~ From the diary of Dr. Henry Orlando Macy, Regimental Surgeon of the 35th United States Colored Infantry, about the burning of Middleton[66]

Built of bricks that were brought over from England, the Middleton family owned this home from 1741 to 1865. Many of the existing supporting buildings were built in 1851. This plantation produced rice, with irrigation provided by dikes that were linked to the Ashley River.

Alligators are now abundant throughout Middleton Plantation. *Photographed at Middleton Plantation.*

William Middleton signed the Ordinance of Secession on December 20, 1860 and later provided the slaves who were used in constructing the defensive works throughout the City of Charleston.

Some of the former slaves from Middleton who returned with the Union army in February 1865 received permission to check on their families.

Before the Union occupation, Middleton packed his wagons full of his possessions and buried some valuables in the yard.[67] The house was burned by Union troops and the gutted walls collapsed during the Earthquake of 1886.

The remains of the Middleton House that survived a fire and an earthquake. *Photographed at Middleton Plantation.*

To return to the Charleston Visitor's Center, turn left onto 61 South. Drive 12 miles to US 17 and turn left onto 17 North. Look for signs to the Visitor's Center.

Many of the support buildings were constructed in 1851. *Photographed at Middleton Plantation.*

A reflection pool at Middleton greets visitors. *Photographed at Middleton Plantation.*

A section of the Middleton home was burned by Union troops in February 1865. *Photographed at Middleton Plantation.*

The Rice Mill was constructed in 1851. *Photographed at Middleton Plantation.*

A replica of a rice boat that was used to navigate dams and dikes in the Low Country. *Photographed at Middleton Plantation.*

The Ashley River as seen from the gardens. *Photographed at Middleton Plantation.*

Rice paddies were saturated with fresh water twice a day by the high tides. *Photographed at Middleton Plantation.*

Slaves attended church services at the chapel every Sunday before the war. *Photographed at Middleton Plantation.*

Chapter Eleven:

JAMES ISLAND...
CHARLESTON'S BACK DOOR

Parrot rifles at Fort Putnam shelled Fort Sumter. *Courtesy of the Library of Congress.*

STOP 1:
GRIMBALL'S LANDING

As you drive in from either direction on US 17, turn onto SC 171/Wesley Drive and go about 9 miles. Turn right on South Grimball Drive and go .5 miles.

On July 16, 1863, Union troops tried to divert Confederate attention from their primary objective, Battery Wagner. Union General Quincy Gilmore planned two feints; an amphibious force moved up the Stono River, threatening the Charleston and Savannah Railroad Bridge. The second force of 3,800 troops, under General Alfred Terry, landed on James Island eight days earlier. They were hoping to draw Southern troops from Battery Wagner and were attacked by General Johnson Hagood's Confederate force of 3,000 troops on July 16. The Confederate attack at Grimball's Landing failed because of lack of reconnaissance and organization. Terry's force accomplished their mission and withdrew the following day.

An estimated number of 3,800 Union troops, under the leadership of General Alfred Terry, beat back a Confederate attack here on July 16, 1863.

Grimball's Landing... Union troops disembarked here as they feinted at the Confederate defenses on James Island July 8, 1863.

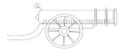

STOP 2:
SOL LEGARE BATTLEFIELD

From Grimball's Landing, return to SC 171 and turn right. Drive 1.3 miles to the next traffic light and turn right. Drive 1.3 miles on Sol Legare Road.

On June 2, 1862, 8,000 Union troops came ashore near the location of Legare's Plantation. This area is located at the southwestern tip of James Island, the so-called 'back door.' Union gunboats supported the landing, firing blindly into the marsh.[68]

In July 1863, this site was where the 54th Massachusetts Infantry engaged in its first combat...only days before the assault on Battery Wagner.

This site was where the 54th Massachusetts experienced its first combat days before their assault on Battery Wagner.

About 8,000 Union troops landed at Sol Legare on June 2, 1862.

STOP 3:
MORRIS ISLAND LIGHTHOUSE

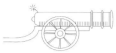 Return to SC 171, turn right, and drive 2.3 miles. At the traffic light, turn left onto East Ashley Avenue and drive 3.3 miles or to the end of the road. From here, you will have to walk 1/4 mile to view the lighthouse.

Union artillery goes into action before the assault on Battery Wagner. *Courtesy of the Library of Congress.*

Battery Wagner

"I shudder as I think of that awful charge. I could hear the sickening thud of case and canister shot slashing through the bodies of the men. How it was possible for a man to reach that fort alive is beyond my comprehension."

~ Colonel Alvin C. Morris, of the 67th Ohio Infantry, witnessing the attack of July 18[69]

The fort was named for Lieutenant Colonel Thomas M. Wagner who was killed during an artillery exercise at Fort Moultrie on July 17, 1862. General Pemberton ordered the construction of the Battery after the Union attacked Secessionville in June 1862 since Battery Gregg was vulnerable. The fort protected the southern part of Morris Island.

Measuring 250 x 100 yards, the Battery was located on an area between the Atlantic and an impassable swamp. The walls were erected of sand and earth. Towering thirty feet above the beach, it was supported by palmetto logs and sandbags. Wagner was armed with fourteen artillery pieces, including a ten-inch Columbiad. The garrison consisted of 1,300 troops. A ditch ten feet wide and five feet deep — and filled with water — protected the exterior of the fort. Additional defenses were buried land mines and sharpened palmetto stakes. At sixty yards wide, the approach to the fort was the only venue for a land attack.

In the summer of 1863, Union Major General Quincy Gilmore had the city of Charleston under his cross hairs. His first step was to capture Morris Island at the mouth of Charleston Harbor. The island was protected by Battery Wagner's garrison of 1,300 Confederate troops, commanded by General William B. Taliaferro. Gilmore believed the fort could be assaulted in the front and then overrun.

The 54th Massachusetts storms Battery Wagner.
Courtesy of the Fort Sumter National Monument.

Battery Wagner would have been located to the right of the Morris Island Lighthouse.

Shown is Confederate artillery behind the sand earthworks of Battery Wagner.

Gilmore spent a week placing over forty artillery pieces to bombard Battery Wagner. The first attack occurred on July 13; the Union forces suffered over two hundred casualties and were driven back, with only a loss of twelve to the defenders. The second operation began on the afternoon of July 18, when the forty guns and seven nearby Union ships shelled the fort for seven hours, in preparation for the planned night assault. Spearheading the assault was the 54th Massachusetts Infantry that was made famous in the motion picture "Glory."[70]

The attack began around 7:30 p.m., as 6,000 Union troops advanced on the 200-yard beach toward Battery Wagner. The Confederates rushed out of their bomb-proofs and manned their positions to repel the assault. As the Union troops reached the parapets, the fighting proved intense. Three regiments managed to occupy a portion of the walls, but they were forced to withdraw after an hour of fierce hand-to-hand combat. Almost every officer was killed, including Colonel Robert Gould Shaw, commander of the 54th Massachusetts; Shaw led six hundred men to the parapet, where he and 272 soldiers became casualties.[71] Repeated Union attacks were repulsed because of additional Rebel artillery support fire from Fort Sumter.[72]

Though the attack was a Union defeat, it proved that African-Americans performed well in battle and allowed for the formation of additional units that helped add numbers to the Union armies and help turn the favor of the war away from the Confederacy.

Today the fort is underwater due to erosion, but its location has been determined to be at the right of the Morris Island Lighthouse.

The attack cost Shaw and his commanding officer, General Strong, their lives. Union losses for the attacks numbered over 1,500 while the Confederates only suffered 174 casualties. The initial bombardment proved little in weakening Wagner's defenses.

Gilmore spent another six weeks maneuvering trenches towards Battery Wagner with the support of guns from the Union navy. On September 6, 1863, the Confederates evacuated Battery Wagner and Morris Island.

Union mortars prepare to bombard Battery Wagner. *Courtesy of the Library of Congress.*

Union mortars fire from captured Battery Wagner into Fort Sumter. *Courtesy of the Library of Congress.*

Battery Wagner...as it appeared after its evacuation in September 1863. *Courtesy of the Library of Congress.*

Battery Gregg

Built before the war, this fort was located on the north end of Morris Island at Cummings Point. A Confederate force of about 1,000 men defended this area. On September 5, 1863, Federal guns started to furiously bombard the battery and during the night they landed troops between Batteries Gregg and Wagner, moving through a creek west of Morris Island on barges. They tried to take Gregg by storming the rear, but were repulsed with heavy losses.

The Confederates fired double canister, stopping the Yankee attack.[73] The Federals continued to shell Battery Gregg while they built trenches toward the fort; once they reached the moat, Beauregard ordered the evacuation of Morris Island[74] and the fort was evacuated on the night of September 6, 1863, with the defenders of Morris Island being evacuated in small boats from Cummings Point after spiking their guns. Renamed Fort Putnam during the Union occupation of Morris Island, it later became the base of Federal heavy artillery that bombarded Fort Sumter.

Confederate troops pinned down the attackers with rifle and canister fire.

Battery Gregg was renamed Fort Putnam after the South evacuated the fortification on September 6, 1863. *Courtesy of the Library of Congress.*

From this point, Citadel Cadets fired on the *Star of the West*, the first shot of the war in January 1861. *Courtesy of the Fort Sumter National Monument.*

STOP 4:
BATTLE OF SECESSIONVILLE
Fort Lamar

Return to SC 171 — the avenue you came in on — and drive about 3.3 miles to the traffic light. Turn right at the light and drive 2.9 miles to Battery Island Road. Turn right and drive .4 miles to Battalion Drive. Turn right and drive .9 miles — the fort will be on your left.

"When within 200 or 300 yards of the earthworks, the left wing came obliquely upon an unforeseen ditch and more as, so that in do advancing it must crowd by it's right flank toward the center. At this moment a terrible fire of grape and musketry opened upon us."

~ Private Stephen Walkley, of the 7th Connecticut Infantry, as he advanced on the Rebel earthworks[75]

This monument honors both the Union and Confederate regiments that fought at the Battle of Secessionville.

Fort Lamar was part of the Confederate defenses that were constructed on James Island beginning in January 1862. The line was anchored by Fort Pemberton on the northwest of the island. Another fortification, Fort Palmetto, protected the Stono River. At Fort Lamar, Secessionville was the center of the defensive line. The construction was carried out by soldiers of the 23rd South Carolina under the command of Colonel Lewis Hatch. At that time, they were the only unit defending James Island. They built a causeway to link the Peninsula with the other defenses along the island; in the center, protecting the causeway, was Fort Lamar or the Tower Battery. The walls were nine feet high and the dry moat was seven feet deep.

Just before dawn on June 16, 1862, Union forces moved toward the Tower Battery and were greeted with fire from a 24-pound gun — the Battle of Secessionville had begun. Accurate Confederate artillery fire broke the ranks of the advancing 8th Michigan Infantry that moved through hedgerows and cotton fields that further impeded their advance. They reached the Battery in piecemeal fashion and were involved in hand-to-hand combat over the earthworks, but were forced to retire. Another wave of Union infantry, the 79th New York Highlanders, tried to rush the walls, but were repulsed by the 9th South Carolina Infantry. These attacks ran along the left side of the causeway.

A third wave of Yankee infantry, the 3rd New Hampshire, attempted a flanking movement during the initial assault, but were bogged down in the marsh and the impassable mud as they tried to move against the Confederate's right side. In the area in front of the parking lot, the 7th Connecticut and 28th Massachusetts moved against the right side of the Battery, but were suppressed by Confederate artillery fire.

Clockwise from top left:

Shown are the earthworks that protected the Confederate right flank.

The earthworks of Fort Lamar trapped members of the 7th Connecticut.

Earthworks of the interior right flank of Fort Lamar.

Shown are additional earthworks at Fort Lamar.

The fighting lasted almost three hours, with 3,500 Union troops being involved in the assault against 1,400 Southern defenders. Union losses were 107 killed, 487 wounded, and eighty-nine missing. The defenders had fifty-two killed, 144 wounded, and eight missing. The Union force evacuated James Island in July and would not return until the summer of 1863.

Two brothers found themselves on opposite sides during the Battle of Secessionville — the Campbells. Both had immigrated to the United States from Scotland during the 1850s, but James Campbell settled in Charleston and his brother Alexander made his home in New York City. During the battle, James was serving with the 1st South Carolina Battalion as a second lieutenant and Alexander was a sergeant with the 79th New York Highlanders. James was the color bearer that planted his flag on the earthworks and held this position until his regiment was forced to withdraw. Neither brother knew that his sibling had been involved in the fighting in the same general vicinity until after the war.

In 1863, a bombproof and magazine were constructed of earth and timber. The Battery was finally completed in the spring of 1864 and was named for Thomas Lamar, who had successfully defended the Tower Battery in June 1862. Lamar died of malaria in October 1862.

Vegetation was planted around the earthworks in 1997 to help prevent the fort's erosion. The fort is now part of the South Carolina Heritage Trust. Under the pavilion, there are brochures for a self-guided tour.

Union forces were bogged down in front of Fort Lamar, unable to breach the walls.

Confederate defenders take aim at an advancing Yankee infantry.

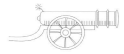

STOP 5:
FORT JOHNSON

From the parking lot, turn right onto Fort Lamar Road and drive .9 miles to Old Military Road. Turn right and drive 1.3 miles. Old Military Road will join Secessionville Road; stay on this route until it intersects with Fort Johnson Road and turn right onto Fort Johnson. Drive 4 miles or to the end of the road and drive into the site.

"On 2nd July we carried Fort Simkins, the Brooke gun battery, and with 135 men (all who had landed) pushed over the parapets of Fort Johnson, and the garrison had actually begun to leave. The battery was in our possession. Nothing but the failure of the other boats to land prevented our capture of the works. All who landed (five boat-loads) were captured. I trust the most thorough investigation will be made, let the responsibility fall where it may."

~ Colonel Henry Hoyt, of the 52nd Pennsylvania Infantry, was captured at Fort Johnson and later wrote as POW at Charleston, August 2, 1864[76]

Secessionist Edmund Ruffin was given the honor of firing one of the first shots against Fort Sumter on April 12, 1861.
Courtesy of the National Archives.

Now a restricted access marine research facility, this fort was constructed during the War of 1812 in response to the British raid on Washington in 1814. After the war, neglect allowed the fort to fall into disrepair and Fort Johnson was abandoned in 1829. The small garrison at Johnson was relocated to Fort Moultrie.

The buildings around Fort Johnson were used as storage facility for the U.S. Engineer's Office in Charleston Harbor. The office was extensively used in the construction of Fort Sumter, serving this purpose until 1860. During this time, sea walls were constructed to protect the site for future fortification.

A small planter's summer village grew nearby called Johnsonville and catered to James Island planters who were trying to avoid malaria and other diseases, but the Confederates occupation of Fort Johnson forced the evacuation of Johnsonville.[77]

On December 26, 1860, the small United States' force at Fort Johnson joined the garrison from Fort Moultrie at Fort Sumter. South Carolina forces quickly occupied the vacant fortification and began erecting earthworks aimed toward Fort Sumter in preparation of a U.S. naval attack against Charleston.

On April 12, 1861, the opening shot against Fort Sumter was the discharge of a mortar battery from Fort Johnson, signaling all Confederate guns to fire on Fort Sumter. The Battery was located on the beach just south of this location; Sumter fell after thirty-four hours of constant bombardment.

When the war commenced, Fort Johnson was the left end of a line of earthworks and batteries that stretched from James Island to the Stono River. By 1863, the fort consisted of large earthen batteries and parapets that covered the Fort Johnson peninsula. Much of Charleston's heavy artillery was located here, dueling with Yankee batteries below James Island.

On July 2, 1864, Federal forces — the 52nd Pennsylvania Infantry, 127th New York Infantry, and the 3rd Rhode Island Artillery — launched an amphibious attack on the fort; initially they encountered some success, but the Confederate defenders were able to repel the attack.[78] They had attacked by using small boats in a creek that ran between the marshes of James and Morris Islands.[79] This landing was part of a major Union effort against Charleston and, while the Confederates beat back the multiple attacks, they sustained heavy losses.

The fort was abandoned February 17, 1865. Elements of the 54th Massachusetts occupied Fort Johnson during the spring and summer of 1865. Then abandoned a second time, it was never fortified again.

On July 2, 1864, Union amphibious forces almost captured Fort Johnson, but their support never materialized

Fort Johnson...as it appeared after Federal forces occupied it in February 1865.
Courtesy of the Library of Congress.

Shown are captured Confederate guns, with a view of Fort Sumter in the distance.
Courtesy of the Library of Congress.

STOP 6:
MCLEOD PLANTATION

325 Country Club Drive

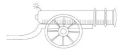 Return to Fort Johnson Road and drive 2.9 miles to Camp Road. Turn right and drive 1.5 miles to Folly Road. Turn right and drive 2.1 miles to Country Club Drive. Turn right — the plantation is the first house on your right.

This plantation grew Sea Island cotton before the war. William McLeod, who purchased the plantation in 1851, owned it, with the present home being constructed in 1856. The main facade was reoriented to the rear of the house in 1925 in the Southern Colonial Revival Style. The 1860 census shows that there were seventy-four slaves here, living in twenty-six cabins. His plantation was one of the largest Sea Island cotton plantations in South Carolina; nine hundred acres were producing one hundred bales of cotton annually.

With the coming of the Civil War and Union occupation of nearby barrier islands, McLeod moved his family to Greenwood. A slave named Steve Forrest was placed in charge of the plantation during the family's absence.

McLeod joined the Charleston Light Dragoons in 1861; the unit was later incorporated into part of the 4th South Carolina Cavalry. From 1862 to 1863, they served with the Department of South Carolina, Georgia and Florida, protecting the Charleston and Savannah Railroad. In March 1864, the 4th was reassigned to the Cavalry Division of the Army of Northern Virginia. McLeod was mortally wounded while serving with the 4th in Virginia.[80]

The home served as headquarters for General Gist's Brigade, whose troops fortified James Island by erecting breastworks to protect the southern approaches to Charleston. An earthwork called Battery Means was constructed at the confluence of Wappoo Creek and the Ashley River.

The McLeod home was later used as a commissary and field hospital until Union forces occupied James Island in February 1865. Dead soldiers were buried at Battery Means. A slave cemetery also exists along the banks of Wappoo Creek.

The McLeod Plantation home was constructed in 1856.

After the Civil War, the McLeod Plantation became the headquarters for the Freedmen's Bureau for the James Island district, but in 1879 the McLeod family were able to regain their property.

In 1918, William Ellis McLeod began raising potatoes, asparagus, and dairy cattle. At his death in 1990, McLeod left the property to the Historic Charleston Foundation. In order to consolidate the holding, Historic Charleston Foundation sold part of the plantation to satisfy claims of others who were beneficiaries in the will.

 To return to Charleston, drive to Folly Road and turn left. Drive .9 miles to the traffic light and turn left onto SC Highway 30.

The Charleston Harbor came under fire in April 1861 — that would continue for another four years. However, the Union Navy was unable to penetrate the harbor's defenses. Today, some of the anchors of that defense are visible and can still be visited.

Chapter Twelve:

CHARLESTON HARBOR

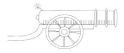

This tour can either begin at Patriot's Point or the Fort Sumter Visitor's Education Center — these are the only two places to catch the ferries. Please check for daily schedules.

CASTLE PINCKNEY

"He made a very minute examination of every department and before leaving, remarked that he found the Castle in better condition, in every respect than any of the other forts, and complimented the garrison on its fine military appearance, and the order and disciplined which prevailed in every department."

~ Mrs. Chicleshee, wife of the commander for the Charleston Zouave Cadets, about Lee's inspection of Castle Pinckney[81]

Constructed just before the outbreak of the War of 1812, this fort is located on Shutes Folly. It was constructed of brick and mortar, but saw no action during the war with Great Britain. Afterwards, the fortification fell into

Charleston residents observe the Union naval attack on Fort Sumter, on April 12, 1861. *Courtesy of the Fort Sumter National Monument.*

disrepair, but was re-garrisoned in 1832 during the Nullification Crisis. After that crisis was quelled, the fort was abandoned and used as a storehouse for military supplies.

In mid-December 1860, the fort was armed with four 42-pounders, fourteen 24-pounders, four eight-inch seacoast howitzers, a ten-inch mortar,

Castle Pinckney was constructed just before the outbreak of the War of 1812.

South Carolina troops seized Castle Pinckney on December 27, 1860.
Courtesy of the Fort Sumter National Monument.

and four light artillery pieces. Accompanying the armor were thirty-four laborers and an ordinance sergeant (and his family).

After the United States transferred its troops from Fort Moultrie to Fort Sumter on December 26, 1860, South Carolina seized all federal property in Charleston. The following day, a South Carolina force of 150 troops, led by future Confederate Generals James J. Pettigrew and Ellison Capers, forced the surrender of Castle Pinckney. The small garrison was forced to join Major Anderson at Fort Sumter. This was the first armed seizure of Federal property by a state government.

The fort was soon occupied by a contingent of the Charleston Zoauve Cadets that occupied the fort during the bombardment of Fort Sumter in April 1861; they later guarded Union prisoners.[82]

After the Battle of First Manassas, Union POWs from the 11th, 69th, and 79th New York and 8th Michigan Infantry Regiments were held here. The Confederates enclosed the lower casemates and converted them into cells. The hotshot furnace was adapted into an oven for food preparation and some of the artillery was relocated around Charleston Harbor.

After these prisoners were exchanged, the fort was converted back to a defensive fortification. Mortars and Columbiads were mounted on the barbette tier of Castle Pinckney; from this position the fort could fire on ships moving towards Charleston from the main harbor channel. This position protected the city from landing parties and protected the wharves and industry around the harbor.

In late January 1863, Confederate ironclads were anchored off Castle Pinckney in an effort to challenge the blockading Union fleet. The fort helped protect the harbor during the Federal assault on April 7 and continued to be active in two additional bombardments on the harbor that occurred between August and December 1863. The Federals continued to hurl more iron into the harbor defenses in the summer of 1864.

Later improvements included earth embankments that were constructed and sodded around the exterior of the fort and the parapet. The Confederates reinforced the exterior fort walls with sand for protection against artillery, especially rifled shells. A lesson learned from the Northern attacks against Fort Sumter.[83]

The Confederates abandoned the fort February 17, 1865, with elements of the United States 21st Colored Infantry soon occupying it. The dirt from the earthworks was pushed into the fort after the war, raising the parade ground. The Federal forces that occupied it used Castle Pinckney as a prison.

The fort was modernized during the Spanish-American War, but it was used later as a light station and storage facility for the Lighthouse Service. Remains of the lighthouse and support buildings still exist.

Today, some of the guns are still in place. It would take a marine crane to remove those 7.5-ton guns. Over the years, relic hunters have taken much of the loose items off the island, which is now the property of the State Ports Authority.

A view of Castle Pinckney as it appeared after Charleston was evacuated.
Courtesy of the Library of Congress.

STEALING OF THE CSS PLANTER

In 1861, the *CSS Planter* moved supplies and weapons between Charleston, Beaufort, and Savannah. Piloted by a slave, Robert Smalls, from nearby Beaufort, the vessel was later used for courier duty, allowing Confederate Brigadier General Rowell Ripley to communicate with the outlaying forts around Charleston Harbor.[84]

On May 13, 1862, Smalls and a few followers stole the *Planter* while the officers were at a gala at Fort Sumter. They were armed with a rifle and a pistol that had been seized from the captain's cabin. Smalls steamed out into the channel, flying the Confederate and Palmetto flags, as they moved down the river.[85]

Confederate pickets ignored them as they passed Castle Pinckney and Forts Johnson and Moultrie. Around sunrise, they passed Fort Sumter. They soon lowered their flags and raised a white sheet, as they raced towards the *USS Onward*. Upon making contact, they were directed to the Union base at Hilton Head.

The *Planter* was then pressed into Union naval service and Smalls was hired as a United States Navy pilot, operating between Charleston and Hilton Head. Smalls also exchanged valuable information about the Confederate defenses on James Island, which led to the Federal attacks at Secessionville in June 1862.[86]

FORT SUMTER

"The firing on that fort will inaugurate a civil war greater than any the world has yet seen...you will lose us every friend at the North. You will wantonly strike a hornet's nest which extends from mountains to ocean. Legions now quiet will swarm out and sting us to death. It is unnecessary. It puts us in the wrong. It is fatal."

~ Robert Toombs, Confederate Secretary of State,
before ordering the attack on Fort Sumter[87]

1860

The fort was named after Thomas Sumter, a Brigadier General of the South Carolina Militia during the Revolutionary War. Construction began on Fort Sumter in 1829, with 70,000 tons of granite brought in from New England to create a man-made island in the middle of the Charleston Harbor. The fortification in 1860, although incomplete, was a pentagon-shaped structure made of masonry. The fort stood fifty feet high during low tide and was designed to hold 650 men and 135 guns on three tiers.

Major Robert Anderson, commander of the garrison at Fort Moultrie, evacuated his command from Moultrie to Sumter on December 26, 1860. Anderson believed Sumter was more defensible, so he spiked his guns and moved under the cover of darkness, infuriating the Republic of South Carolina.

Though the Union garrison had moved to Fort Sumter for better protection, the occupation had its drawbacks, including a limited amount of supplies — only four months worth was available. Major Anderson reported the situation to Washington that in order to hold Sumter he would need additional supplies and reinforcements.[88]

Fort Sumter was under bombardment April 12-13, 1861.
Courtesy of the Fort Sumter National Monument.

1861

Major Robert Anderson commanded Fort Sumter at the outbreak of the war. *Courtesy of the National Archives.*

Washington, not wanting to provoke South Carolina or escalate the situation, hired a private steamer, the *Star of the West*, to ferry two hundred troops and supplies to Fort Sumter. They left New York City on January 5, arriving four days later at the entrance of Charleston Harbor. Cadets from the Citadel, stationed on nearby Morris Island, fired on the *Star of the West*, but they were out of range. The firing forced the steamer to reverse its course for New York City. The captain of the *Star of the West* made that decision when he realized that there was no supporting fire from Sumter. Anderson had ordered his guns manned, but was reluctant to fire. It was Washington's policy of not trying to provoke the Southerners; they handled this situation very lightly until Lincoln was sworn in as President.

A new plan was drafted in February; it called for a force on light-draft steamers, loaded with additional troops and provisions, to run past the Confederate batteries, but the steamers would had to have been evacuated upon the mission's completion. It was not acted upon.[89]

The Confederates continued to position guns around the Charleston Harbor. There were batteries at Fort Johnson, on James Island, Cumming's Point, and the northern end of Morris Island. Sullivan's Island was further strengthened by mortar batteries to the east of Fort Moultrie. There was a floating battery of long-range guns off the west end of Sullivan's Island. The guns at Fort Moultrie had been repaired and remounted. There were mortar batteries near Mount Pleasant and Castle Pinckney.[90]

With the formation of the Confederate States of America on February 7, 1861, the new nation sent representatives to Washington in an effort to purchase Fort Sumter, but negotiations stalled and Lincoln later rejected any offerings based on the fact that the Confederacy was not a legal nation.

Lincoln was informed just after his inauguration that Anderson had only six weeks of supplies; his provisions would be exhausted in mid-April. Lincoln met with advisors who voiced that Sumter could not be reinforced because of inadequate forces. Federal officials, through channels, communicated with Southern officials that Sumter would be evacuated.[91]

Lincoln, however, had other thoughts: on April 6, he ordered a naval expedition to replenish Fort Sumter's stores with no reinforcements. An emissary from Washington was sent to Governor Pickens of South Carolina informing him of Lincoln's orders. Pickens forwarded the information to Confederate President Jefferson Davis.[92]

Fort Sumter was not yet completed when Anderson occupied it on December 26, 1860.

Davis met with his cabinet; they thought that firing on the expedition would cause war and alienate any allies they had in the North. Davis looked at the crisis from a different perception: the world was watching and Lincoln had politically outmaneuvered him. Davis immediately sent a message to General Beauregard, commander the Confederate forces in Charleston, demanding that Anderson surrender the fort. Anderson replied that if the Confederate artillery did not batter Sumter, they would be starved out in a matter of days.[93] Davis was fearful of the additional navy guns that were steaming toward Charleston, so he ordered the reduction of the fort before the fleet arrived. Beauregard later sent a party under a flag of truce informing Anderson to evacuate or he would be forced to fire; Anderson refused, so at 4:30 a.m. on April 12 Confederate guns from around the harbor roared.

The first shot was fired by Virginia secessionist Edmund Ruffin, who four years later would take his own life instead of living under the Stars and Stripes again. Citizens of Charleston sat on rooftops observing the exchange of the thunderous artillery, during which the flagpole had been damaged. The Confederates paused thinking the garrison was going to surrender, but a Union sergeant tacked the flag back and the Confederates cheered him for the courage he had shown.[94]

Two days later, after the Confederates had fired 4,000 rounds at Sumter, Anderson surrendered. There had been no casualties during the engagement, but two of Anderson's soldiers were killed during a salute to the colors, which was soon ended.

The end result was a full-fledged war between the United States and the Confederate States. Lincoln immediately called for 75,000 volunteers to put down the rebellion — a plea that forced four other states out of the Union.

Charleston as viewed through one of Fort Sumter's casemates.

The Confederate Stars and Bars flies over Fort Sumter after its capitulation.
Courtesy of the Fort Sumter National Monument.

This monument honors the Union defenders of Fort Sumter.

1862

The north wall facing Fort Moultrie. During 1862, the fort was the scene of many social gatherings that were attended by both soldiers and civilians alike.

This damaged wall was photographed in 1865. *Courtesy of the Library of Congress.*

1863

On April 7, 1863, a Union naval force of nine ironclads attacked Fort Sumter; it was thought that the action would weaken Sumter's defenses, allowing Union infantry to land and capture the fort. These ironclads had previously attacked Savannah's Fort McAllister to gain experience in attacking a fixed fortification.[95]

The naval force was commanded by Rear Admiral Samuel Du Pont; Major General David Hunter commanded the infantry assault force that had assembled on the nearby coastal islands, Folly and North Edisto. The naval attack failed and the landings were cancelled. Du Pont's force endured serious punishment and lost one of its ironclads to accurate Confederate fire.

On August 17, the newly erected Union batteries on Morris Island pounded Fort Sumter. Within a week, the fort's brick walls were in ruins, but the garrison refused to surrender and continued to repair and strengthen its defenses. Confederate guns at Fort Moultrie and other strongholds in the harbor returned fire, but the Federals continuously bombarded Sumter throughout the year.

After the complete Confederate evacuation of Batteries Gregg and Wagner on the night of September 6-7, Union General Quincy Gilmore ordered a 400-man strong contingent of marines and sailors to seize Fort Sumter, but the attack was easily repulsed.

The 'Dingie Plan' was conceived in October 1863. The idea was to have multiple twelve-men crews in specially made boats from New York City attack Fort Sumter at night. It was hoped that this attack would surprise and capture the garrison. Training began on St. Helena Island, near Beaufort in October. After extensive training, the troops of the 7th Connecticut Infantry were ordered to Folly Island to construct scaling ladders. The plan was abandoned in mid-November.[96]

This Confederate infantry defeated a Union amphibious assault on the night of September 6-7, 1863.

Additional damage from Union guns occurred from nearby Morris Island.

A view of the damage done from the constant Union shelling in the autumn of 1863.

Union monitors unsuccessfully attacked Fort Sumter on April 7, 1863.
Courtesy of the Fort Sumter National Monument.

Field pieces were positioned in the wake of any Union amphibious attack. *Courtesy of the Library of Congress.*

1864

In the summer of 1864, Union Major General John Foster, newly appointed commander of the Department of the South, believed that Fort Sumter could be taken under certain circumstances. Foster pulverized the fort for two months with out any results, so the operation was tabled. Many of Foster's troops were transferred to Virginia for operations against Richmond and Petersburg. The limited resources kept Foster from renewing any additional attacks in the second half of 1864.

A powder monkey is shown aboard the *USS New Hampshire*, which was part of the blockading fleet around Charleston. *Courtesy of the National Archives.*

More damage, caused by the constant artillery from Yankee guns, took place on Morris Island.

1865

It is thought that over 7 million pounds of ammunition was fired at Fort Sumter during the war. The Confederates only suffered 319 casualties through the entire war.

The fort was evacuated on February 17, as Sherman's troops approached Charleston from the South. On April 14, Robert Anderson, promoted to general, raised the flag four years to the day after he lowered the flag to Confederate forces.[97]

An aerial view of Fort Sumter's defenses in 1865. *Courtesy of the Library of Congress.*

WORKS CITED AND OTHER RESOURCES

[1] http://militaryhistory.suite101.com/article.cfm/the_confederate_marine_corps

[2] Tagg, Larry. *The Generals of Gettysburg*. Campbell, California: Savas Publishing Company, 1998; page 64

[3] http://quotes.liberty-tree.ca/quotes_by/john+c.+calhoun

[4] http://americancivilwar.50megs.com/JohnsonDiv/NightAttack.html

[5] Ripley, Warren, editor. *Siege Train: The Journal of a Confederate Artilleryman in the Defense of Charleston*. Columbia, South Carolina: University of South Carolina Press, 1986; p. xviii

[6] *South Carolina Historical Magazine*. South Carolina Historical Society, 1904.

[7] Coy, Mary Clark. *The Civil War Walking History Book*. Charleston, South Carolina: self-published, 2003; page 16

[8] Time-Life Books Editors. *Charleston: Voices of the Civil War*. Alexandria, Virginia: Time-Life Books, 1997; page 140

[9] D'Arcy, David and Ben Mammina. *Civil War Tours of the Low Country*. Atglen, Pennsylvania: Schiffer Publishing, Ltd., 2008; page 41

[10] *Charleston: Voices of the Civil War*, p. 136

[11] Williams, Harry T. *P. G. T. Beauregard, Napoleon in Gray*. Baton Rouge, Louisiana: Louisiana State University Press, 1955; page 191

[12] Warren, Ezra J. *Generals in Gray: Lives of Confederate Commanders*. Baton Rouge, Louisiana: Louisiana State University Press, 1959; page 44

[13] www.spartacus.schoolnet.co.uk/USASgrimkeS.html.

[14] Coy, p. 1

[15] www.furman.edu/president/42.html.

[16] *Charleston: Voices of the Civil War*, p. 238

[17] Coy, p. 21

[18] Ibid

[19] Poston, Jonathon H. *The Buildings of Charleston: A Guide to the City's Architecture*. Columbia, South Carolina: South Carolina University Press, 1997; page 55

[20] Walker, C. I. *Rolls and Historical Sketch of the Tenth Regiment: South Carolina Volunteers in the Army of the Confederate States*. Charleston, South Carolina: Walker, Everest & Cogswell Printers, 1881; page 119

[21] Poston, p. 110

[22] Ibid, 104

[23] Coy, p. 10

[24] Poston, p. 150

[25] "Civil War Journal: Destiny at Fort Sumter" (video). Greystone Communications, 1993.

[26] Coy, p. 9

[27] Wiley, Bell Irvin. *Confederate Women*. Westport, Connecticut, and London, England: Greenwood Press, 1975; page 9

[28] Coy, p. 9

[29] Ibid

[30] *Charleston: Voices of the Civil War*, p. 140

[31] Coy, p. 8

[32] Poston, p. 64

[33] Crooks Jr., Daniel J. *Lee in the Low Country: Defending Charleston and Savannah 1861-1862*. Charleston, South Carolina: History Press, 2008; page 66

[34] www.historynet.com/immortal-600-prisoners-under-fire-at-charleston-harbor-during-the-american-civil-war.html/3

[35] Ibid

[36] Phelps, W. Chris. *Charlestonians in War: The Charleston Battalion*. Gretna, Louisiana: Pelican Publishing Company, 2004; page 31

[37] Ibid, 62

[38] Ibid, 95

[39] Ibid, 122

[40] Poston, p. 86

[41] Angle, Paul. *The Nation Divided: The Civil War Before and After*. Greenwich, Connecticut: Fawcett World Library, 1964; page 98

[42] Poston, p. 87

Anderson, now a brigadier general, hoists the flag over Fort Sumter on April 14, 1865.
Courtesy of the Library of Congress.

[43] Coy, p. 23

[44] Burton, E. Milby. *The Siege of Charleston, 1861-1865*. Columbia, South Carolina: University of South Carolina Press, 1970; page 309

[45] http://www.batsonsm.tripod.com/b/reg1g.html

[46] Pember-Yates, Phoebe. *A Southern Woman's Story: Life in Confederate Richmond*. Ed. Bell Irvin Wiley. Jackson, Tennessee: McCovat-Mercer Press, 1959; page 131
[47] D'Arcy, David. *Civil War Walking Tour of Savannah*. Atglen, Pennsylvania: Schiffer Publishing, Ltd., 2006; page 66
[48] Phelps, 21
[49] Ibid, 31
[50] Ibid, 40
[51] Ibid, 51
[52] Ibid, 117
[53] Ibid, 144
[54] Cochran, Hamilton. *Blockade Runners of the Confederacy*. Indianapolis, Indiana, and New York, New York: The Bobbs-Merrill Company, 1958; page 158
[55] *Charleston: Voices of the Civil War*, p. 84
[56] Burton, p. 169
[57] Ibid, 44
[58] Kloeppel, James E. *Danger Beneath the Waves: A History of the Confederate Submarine H. L. Hunley*. Orangeburg, South Carolina: Sandlapper Publishing, Inc, 1997; p. 28
[59] Ibid, 9
[60] Ibid, 23
[61] Ibid, 61
[62] www.fullbooks.com/History-of-Kershaw-s-Brigade9.html
[63] http://www.home.freeuk.net/gazkhan/micah.html
[64] Warren, p. 257
[65] Time-Life Books Editors. *Charleston: Voices of the Civil War*; page 147
[66] Macy, Henry Orlando, Dr. "Dairy Excerpts: Regimental Surgeon, 35th US Colored Infantry," Drayton Hall Archives.
[67] Drayton Hall Archives
[68] Conner, T. D. *War on the South Coast 1861-1865*. Savannah, Georgia: Writeplace Press, 2004.
[69] *Charleston: Voices of the Civil War*, p. 100
[70] http://www.awod.com/cwchas/wagner.html
[71] Burchard, Peter. *One Gallant Rush: Robert Gould Shaw and His Brave Black Regiment*. New York, New York: St Martin's Press, 1965; page 139
[72] http://en.wikipedia.org/wiki/Fort_Wagner
[73] Richardson, Charles B. *Southern History of the War: The Third Year of the War*. New York, New York: Edgar A. Pollars, 1865; page 93 (*Digitized August 9, 2006, original from Harvard University.*)
[74] *The Illustrated London News*, vol. 43, no. 1223, p. 303, September 26, 1863. (*www.civilwaralbum.com/misc9/morris_island1a.html*)
[75] Walkley, Stephen. *History of the Seventh Connecticut Volunteer Infantry: 1861-1865, Hawley's Brigade, Terry's Division, 10th Army Corps*. Southington, Connecticut: 1905; page 50
[76] Mott, Smith B. *The Campaigns of the Fifty-Second Regiment, Pennsylvania Volunteers*. Lippincott, Philadelphia: University of California Online, 2007; page 157
[77] www.awod.com/cwchas/johnson.html
[78] Ibid
[79] Mott, p. 158
[80] www.researchonline.net/sccw/unit74.html
[81] Crooks, p. 86
[82] www.geocities.com/cmp_csa/CastlePickney.html
[83] Ibid
[84] D'Arcy, *Civil War Tours of the Low Country*, p. 102
[85] Connor, 89
[86] D'Arcy, *Civil War Tours of the Low Country*, p. 102
[87] Foote, Shelby. *The Civil War A Narrative: Fort Sumter to Perryville*. New York, New York: Vintage Books, 1986; p. 47
[88] www.historynet.com/magazines/american_civil_war/3032636.html
[89] Ibid
[90] Jones, Samuel. *The Siege of Charleston*. New York, New York: Neale Publishing Company, 1911; page 34
[91] Foote, p. 46
[92] Ibid, 47
[93] Ibid, 48
[94] Ibid, 50
[95] D'Arcy, *Civil War Walking Tour of Savannah*, p. 140
[96] Walkley, p. 113
[97] www.experiencefestival.com/a/Fort_Sumter_-_18631865/id/1401315

Other Resources

Fremantle, Lt. Col. Arthur. *Three Months in the Southern States, April-July 1863*. Westport, Connecticut: Negro University Press, 1970.
Girard, Charles. *A Visit to the Confederate States of America in 1863: Memoir Addressed to His Majesty Napoleon III*. Ed. William Stanley Hoole. Tuscaloosa, Alabama: Confederate Publishing Inc, 1962.
Manigault, Edward. *Siege Train: The Journal of A Confederate Artilleryman in the Defense of Charleston*. Ed. Warren Ripley. Columbia, South Carolina: University of South Carolina Press, 1986.
Pollard, Edgar A. *Southern History of the War. The Third Year of the War*. New York, New York: Charles B. Richardson, 1865.
Scheibert, Captain Justus. *Seven Months in the Rebel States During the North American War, 1863*. Ed. William Stanley Hoole. Tuscaloosa, Alabama: Confederate Publishing Company Inc., 1958.
Time-Life Book Editors. *Shenandoah, 1864: Voices of the Civil War*. Alexandria, Virginia: Time-Life Books, 1997.
White, Henry Alexander. *Robert E. Lee and the Southern Confederacy 1807-1870*. New York, New York, and London, England: G. P. Putnam's Sons, 1909.
Wise, Stephen R. *Lifeline of the Confederacy: Blockade Running During the Civil War*. Columbia, South Carolina: University of South Carolina Press, 1991.
www.battleofolustee.org/7th_ct_inf.html

Union troops were repulsed with heavy losses on September 5, 1863, while assaulting Battery Gregg.

INDEX

7th Connecticut Infantry Regiment, 126, 127, 138
8th Michigan Infantry Regiment,126, 134
8th Texas Cavalry Regiment, 114
67th Ohio Infantry Regiment, 123

Aiken House, 12
Aiken-Rhett House, 10
Alston, Charles, 6
American Diver, 98
Anderson, Major Robert, 7, 104, 105, 134, 136, 137, 140
Andersonville, Georgia, 64
Anti-Slavery Society, 42
Appomattox Court House, 102
Army of...
    Mississippi, 20, 37
    Northern Virginia, 5, 17, 43, 74, 99, 101, 102, 114, 131
    Potomac, the, 15, 26, 27
    Tennessee, 17, 20, 41, 45, 49, 60, 92, 101, 102
Ashley Hall, 85
Ashley River, 28, 111, 116-119
Atlantic Ocean, 123
Augusta, Georgia, 89

Bachman, Doctor John, 63
Baltimore, Maryland, 77
Bamberg, South Carolina, 22
Battery Gregg, 123, 125, 138
Battery Marshall, 102, 108
Battery Means, 131
Battery, The, 22
Battery Wagner, 64, 66, 74, 94, 102, 121-125, 138
Battle of...
    Antietam, 19, 99
    Atlanta, 5, 41, 45, 114
    Aversboro, 84, 101
    Bentonville, 28
    Cedar Run, 99
    Chancellorsville, 15, 17
    Chattanooga, 41, 60
    Chickamauga, 41, 45, 99, 114

Cold Harbor, 88, 92, 102
Falling Waters, 43
Franklin, 20, 41
Fredericksburg, 14, 17, 99
Gettysburg, 15, 17, 34, 41, 43, 99, 101
Honey Hill, 12
Kingston, 45
McClellanville, 25
Murfreesboro, 114
Perryville, 45
Resaca, 20
Secessionville, 41, 66, 102, 126, 128, 135
Seven Pines, 43
Sharpsburg, 17, 99
Shiloh, 31, 37, 114
Sol Legare, 122
Spotsylvania, 92
Wilderness, 92, 99
Yellow Tavern, 17
Beaufort, South Carolina, 42, 53, 135, 138
Beauregard, Gen. Pierre G. T., 6, 10, 31, 37, 40, 52, 53, 59, 60, 84, 98, 125, 137
Bee, General Barnard, 79
Bee, James Ladson, 88
Bee, John Stock, 88
Bee, William C., 7, 88
Bee Range, 88
Beefsteak Raid, 17
Bermuda, 85
Bethany Cemetery, 101
Bible Depository, 58
Bluffton, South Carolina, 12
Boone Hall Plantation, 109-110
Brady, Matthew, 116
Breach's Inlet, 9
Buchanan, President James, 7
Bunker Hill, Virginia, 43

C. D. Franke Company, 81
California, 25, 86
Calhoun, John C., 7, 17, 68, 86
Camden, South Carolina, 99
Campbell, Alexander, 70, 128

Capers, Gen. Ellison, 6, 41, 78, 134
Carolinas Campaign, 12
Casper Christian Schutt House, 48
Castle Pinckney, 79, 133-136
Cathedral of St. John Baptist, 57, 61
Chambersburg, Pennsylvania, 17
Charleston and Savannah Railroad, 12, 20, 121, 131
Charleston City Hall, 30
Charleston County Court House, 29
Charleston Courier, 52
Charleston Mercury, 2, 31, 86, 91
Charleston Museum, 20
Charleston, South Carolina, 5-7, 15, 16, 19, 20, 22, 25-27, 29, 31, 37, 39, 40, 42-44, 47, 49, 53, 55, 56, 58, 64, 70, 73, 74, 79, 84. 85, 87, 91, 92, 95, 98-100, 102, 105, 107, 110, 112-114, 118, 123, 128-130, 132, 133, 135
Charleston Visitors Center, 9, 98
Chestnut, Mary Boykin, 7, 54, 59
Chimborazo Hospital, 77
Circular Congregational Church, 66
Citadel, 16, 41, 99, 112, 125, 136
Columbia, South Carolina, 17, 32, 41, 45, 63, 76
Confederate Congress, 85
Confederate Hospitals, 13, 18, 41, 94, 112
Confederate Monument, 21
Confederate Museum, 72
Confederate States of America, 10, 31, 35, 62, 68, 85, 95, 105, 124, 136
Congregation Beth Elohm, 76
Conner, General James, 6, 99
Cooper, George W., 91, 93
CSS David, 56
CSS Hunley, 22, 56, 98, 100, 107, 108
CSS Planter, 135
CSS Stono, 53
Cummings Point, 125, 136
Cussler, Clive, 98

Dalgren, Admiral John A., 7
Davis, President Jefferson, 6, 10, 60, 136, 137

Department of...
    Mississippi & East Louisiana, 114
    North Carolina & Southeast Virginia, 37, 84
    South Carolina, Georgia & Florida, 12, 37, 45, 92, 101, 102, 131
    South, the, 27, 140
DeSaussure, General Wilmot, 6, 49
Dickert, Captain D. Augustus, 99
District Court House, 44
Dixon, Lieutenant George, 6, 107
Drayton Family, 39, 114
Drayton Hall, 111, 113-115
Drayton, Thomas Fenwick, 6, 32
Drayton, Percival, 7, 32
Drewery's Bluff, Virginia, 79
Dupont, Rear Admiral Samuel, 138
Durham, North Carolina, 5, 12, 102, 114

Edisto Island, South Carolina, 99
Edmonston-Alston House, 52
Edmonston, Charles, 53
Elliot, Lieuetenant Colonel Stephen, 37

Fayetteville, North Carolina, 107
First Louisiana Hospital, 112
First Scots Presbyterian Church, 35
Florence, South Carolina, 64
Folly Island, South Carolina, 138
Foster, General John, 7, 91, 140
Fort Johnson, 129, 130, 135, 136
Fort Lamar, 126-128
Fort McAllister,138
Fort Moultrie, 99, 101, 103-106, 123, 129, 134-136, 138
Fort Pulaski, 85, 91
Fort Putnam, 120, 125
Fort Simkins, 129
Fort Sumter, 16, 20, 29, 37, 40, 49, 52, 53, 54, 59, 84, 91, 99, 102, 104-106, 110, 120, 124, 125, 129, 130, 133-140
Francis, Jacob, 65
Fraser & Company, 48, 85, 98
Fraser, Trenholm & Company, 85
Fraser, John, 7, 48

Freedmen's Bureau, 131
French Protestant Church, 67

Gavelston, Texas, 25
Georgia Infantry Regiments...
    27th and 28th, 79
Georgetown, South Carolina, 20, 24, 53
Gilmore, Gen. Quincy, 7, 40, 121, 123, 124, 138
Gist, General, 131
Glassell, Lieutenant William, 56
Grant, General Ulysses S., 5, 15
Great Compromise, The, 17
Great Fire of December 1861, 57, 59, 61, 62, 66
Greenwood, South Carolina, 131
Grimball's Landing, 20. 121
Grimke, Angelina and Sarah, 7, 42, 116

Hagood, General Johnson, 79, 121
Hamilton-Bennett House, 89
Hampton, General Wade, 6, 16, 17, 51, 75, 79, 101
Hatch, General John, 7, 26, 27, 68, 113
Hatch, Colonel Lewis, 126
Hayne, Paul, 89
Heth, General Henry, 43
Heyward-Washington House, 42
Hilton Head, South Carolina, 32, 113, 135, 138
Historic Charleston Foundation, 131
Holmes, Emma, 88
Houston, Texas, 114
Hoyt, Colonel Henry, 129
Huger, Alfred, 6, 62
Huger, Daniel E., 38
Hunley, Horace, 98

Inglis Arch House, 47
Ingraham, Commodore Duncan, 95

Jackson, President Andrew, 17
James Island, South Carolina, 20, 66, 70, 79, 120, 122, 126, 128, 130, 131, 135, 136

Jenkins, General Micah, 6, 99
John Ravenal Home, 56
Johns' Island, South Carolina, 12, 53
Johnson, President Andrew, 15
Johnsonville, South Carolina, 129
Johnston, General Albert S., 37
Johnston, General Joseph E., 17
Jones, General Samuel, 6
Jordan, Thomas, 98
Joseph Manigault House, 20

Kings Mountain Military School, 99

Ladies Memorial Association, 34, 41
Lake Ponchartrain, 98
Lamar, Thomas, 128
Lather, Colonel Richard, 24
Laughton, William, 87
Laurel Grove Cemetery, 77
Lee, Gen. Robert E., 6, 17, 32, 53, 59
Legare's Plantation, 122
Lincoln, President Abraham, 7, 42, 44, 68, 136
Liverpool, Great Britain, 85
Longstreet, General James, 99, 101
Lynch, Bishop Patrick, 7, 61

Macy, Dr. Henry Orlando, 118
Magnolia Cemetery, 20, 34, 41, 49, 85, 97, 99
Magnolia Plantation & Gardens, 116, 117
Manassas, First Battle of, 16, 37, 79, 99, 134
Manassas, Second Battle of, 14, 74, 99
Manigault, Arthur and Edward, 6, 20
Marion Square, 16
Marshall, Reverent Alexander, 68
Massachusetts Infantry Regiments...
    Twenty-Eighth, 126
    Fifty-Fourth, 29, 64, 122-124, 130
Marx Cohen House, 28
Meade, Gen. George G., 7, 15, 26, 127
Memminger, Secretary Christopher, 6, 85
Mexican War, 20, 37, 99
McCrady, Edward, 7, 74
McGrath, Judge Andrew, 44
McLeod Plantation, 131
McLeod, William, 131
Middleton Plantation, 23, 99, 118, 119

Middleton, William, 118
Miles Brewerton House, 26
Mills House Hotel, 51, 53, 59
Mills, Otis, 51
Mobile, Alabama, 98
Mobile Bay, Alabama, 98
Montgomery, Alabama, 105
Morgan, Mid-Shipman James Morris, 85
Morris, Colonel Alvin C., 123
Morris Island Lighthouse, 123-124
Morris Island, South Carolina, 29, 40, 49, 79, 88, 91, 112, 123-125, 130, 136, 139, 140
Moultrie, Colonel William, 105
Mount Pleasant, South Carolina, 103, 136
Mount Royal Plantation, 110

Nassau, Bahamas, 85
Nathaniel Ingraham House, 51
Nathaniel Russell House, 36
New Hampshire Units...
    Infantry regiments: Third, 126
New Orleans, Jackson and Mississippi Railroad, 37
New Orleans, Louisiana, 37, 98
New Tabernacle Fourth Baptist Church, 11
New York City, 24, 73, 100, 128, 136
New York Infantry Regiments...
    11th and 69th, 134
    56th, 118
    79th Highlanders, 126, 128, 134
    127th, 130
North Edisto Island, South Carolina, 138
Nullification Crisis, 17, 68, 133

Old Marine Hospital, 94
Old Slave Mart, 58
Ogeechee River, 84
Old Exchange Building, 46
Old Jail, 64
Ordinance of Secession, 50, 63, 86, 118

Payas-Mordecai House, 34
Pember, Phoebe Yates, 77
Pemberton, General John, 6, 123
Peninsula Campaign, 14, 16, 99, 101, 102
Pennsylvania Units...
    Infantry Regiment: 52nd, 129-130
Petersburg, Siege of, 92, 149

Petersburg, Virginia, 5, 43, 79, 102
Pettigrew, Gen. James Johnston, 6, 43, 79, 134
Petigru, James Louis, 7, 43
Pickens, Governor, 29, 136
Pocotalico, South Carolina, 101
Porcher, Francis, 50
Porcher-Simonds House, 50
Port Royal Sound, 32
Powder Magazine, 69
Pringle, John, 53

Ramsay, Major David, 66
Ravenal, St. Julien, 7, 56
Revolutionary War, 105, 116, 135
Rhett, Alfred, 6, 84
Rhett, Robert Barnwell, 84
Rhett, Robert Barnwell Sr., 7, 86
Rhode Island Units...
    Artillery regiments: Third, 130
Richmond, Virginia, 5, 17, 43, 77, 99, 149
Ripley, General Sabine, 6, 99
Ruffin, Edmund, 129, 137
Ryan, John, 58

St. Helena Island, South Carolina, 138
St. John's Lutheran Church, 63
St. John's Reformed Episcopal Church, 80
St. Lawrence Cemetery, 102
St. Michael's Episcopal Church, 32
St. Patrick O'Donnell House, 25
St. Paul's Catholic Church, 76
St. Philip's Episcopal Church, 17, 45, 68
St. Stephen's Church, 80
Savannah, Georgia, 12, 77, 84, 115
Saxton, General Rufus, 53
Sebrig-Aimar House, 83
Second Battle of Fort Fisher, 79
Second Presbyterian Church, 19
Seige of Vicksburg, 89
Shaw, Colonel Robert Gould, 124
Shenandoah Valley, Virginia, 94
Sherman, General William T., 5, 22, 64, 68, 92, 100, 101, 140
Shutes Folly, 133
Sickles, General Daniel, 7, 14, 15
Simms, William Gilmore, 22
Simons, General James, 29
Simons, General Samual Wragg, 29, 92
Smalls, Robert, 7, 135

Smyth, Corporal Augustine, 32
Snowden, Amarintha, 41
Snowden, Williams, 7, 41
South Carolina College, 16, 99
South Carolina Heritage Trust, 128
South Carolina Sea Grant Consortium, 79
South Carolina Units...
    Artillery regiments:
        3rd Battalion, 114;
        Buist's Battery, 107;
        German Light Artillery, 101;
        Marion, 29
    Cavalry regiments:
        3rd and 4th, 12, 92, 100;
        Charleston Light Dragoons, 92, 99, 131
    Infantry regiments:
        1st, 102;
        1st Battalion, 128;
        1st Rifles, 100;
        5th, 99;
        9th, 126;
        10th, 20, 126;
        12th, 43;
        23rd, 126;
        24th, 41;
        25th, 29;
        27th, 102;
        Charleston Battalion, 66, 102;
        Charleston Zouave Cadets, 133;
        Hampton's Legion, 16, 79, 101;
        Palmetto Battalion, 119;
        Union Light of the 17th, 66;
        Washington Light, 31, 79, 99
South Newport, South Carolina, 12
Star of the West, 112, 124, 136
Stono River, 53, 121, 126, 130
Strong, General, 124
Stuart, General James Ewell Brown, 17
Sullivan's Island, South Carolina, 41, 98, 136
Summerville, South Carolina, 116
Sumter, General Thomas, 135

Taliaferro, General William B., 6, 123
Terry, General Alfred, 121
Timrod, Henry, 31
Toombs, Robert, 135
Tower Battery, 126, 128

Trenholm, Edward, 87
Trenholm, George Alfred, 7, 28, 85-87
Trinity United Methodist Church, 41, 78
Tullahoma, Tennessee, 41
Tyrell County, North Carolina, 43

Union Prisons, 91, 94
United Confederate Veterans, 41, 45
United States Colored Units...
    2nd Artillery Regiments, 113
    21st Infantry Regiment, 134
    35th Infantry Regiment, 118
United States Custom House, 70
United States Postal Service, 77
University of Georgia, 31
University of North Carolina, 43
USS Housatonic, 56, 98, 107
USS Isaac P. Smith, 53
USS Meredita, 95
USS New Hampshire, 140
USS New Ironsides, 56, 98
USS Onward. 135

Valk House, 61

Wagner, Lt Colonel Thomas M., 123
Walker, Evans & Cogswell Building, 6, 45
Walker, Lt. Colonel Cornelius Irvine, 6, 45, 68
Walkley, Private Stephen, 126
Wappoo Creek, 131
Washington, DC, 104, 129, 136
Washington Park, 30
Weld, Theodore, 42
White Point Gardens, 21
William Ravenal Home, 54
William Roper House, 55
Williams, George W., 73
Wilmington, North Carolina, 79